The Editor's Wastebasket

Mario G. Fumarola

Illustrations by
Robert Cimbalo
Charles R. Favreault, Jr.

The Editor's Wastebasket
Copyright 2015
ISBN 978-1-94378917-7

Taylor and Seale Publishing, LLC
Daytona Beach Shores, Florida 32118
888-866-8248

Dedication

The dedication is to you, the reader, as you make yourself your own bonafide editor of printed material. The following pages convey a roller coaster ride, stepping onto and off soap boxes, in an attempt to seek lofty answers to issues and then back down to ground level; mounting and dismounting a toy rocking horse that constantly moves while the rider doesn't move an inch. As you dig into this collage of written pieces, you might find a memory or an experience that you may have lived and now remember. There are disappointments and failures, victories, and a quiet love that a sensitive heart will see and feel, and you will embrace it and know it well.

It is hoped that **you**, the *reader–editor,* will also find some humor. We must never forget to listen always for the innocent laughter of children. One of Tony's favorite classical pieces is the *1812 Overture* by Tchaikovsky, because he anticipates the sound of the bells tolling even over the din of artillery fire. The laughter of the innocent and the peal of bells can easily become a haven for hope.

Comments

Amici e amici di amici (Friends and friends of friends)

The Editor's Wastebasket is author Mario Fumarola's journey of prose through America's urban landscape of the 20th century experience as the son of Italian immigrants, of a childhood enmeshed in poverty and cultural intolerance, yet, at the same time, of a fulfillment among the close bonds made among family members and friends. Mario brings the experiences of American assimilation through the lens of a proud Italian American; a man who cannot escape a love for his family's homeland. Italy and America come together in *The Editor's Wastebasket* like a holiday meal, a mix of traditional Italian and new American fare in the way of engaging stories and observations. Mario's writing flows effortlessly from one experience to another, like a river of epiphanies that define the human experience.

I am the editor of PRIMO magazine and I enthusiastically recommend your reading *The Editor's Wastebasket*. It is an exceptional book that brings poetry to the hardscrabble lives of our immigrant ancestors and their children, our fathers and mothers, who became the Greatest Generation.

Truby Chiaviello, Editor, *PRIMO* Magazine

The Editor's Wastebasket is a collage of memories and meditations (some sad, some sweet) of the past (the Italian-American enclave of East Utica, NY), the present (old age in Pennsylvania), and thoughts of his kids in the world of the new technologies. Taken together, they are consistently charming and touching.

Dr. Eugene P. Nassar, Professor of English,
Emeritus Utica College, and founder of the
Ethnic Heritage Studies Center, Utica College.

If you can't have an *espresso* and *grappa* with Mario Fumarola sometime, then you'd better read this book. He's someone worth listening to, not because he knows it all, but because he knew it when: from sometime after the invention of electricity and before computers—when *pasta fagioli* wasn't an appetizer and Utica, New York was a home to a mix of immigrants whose kids would go on to change the world. But, like Tony, Mario's narrator says, the world never really changes, no matter how hard we try. It just stays human, and it's Mario's version of humanity that should make you think, laugh, and if not cry, then certainly sigh at all this storyteller has witnessed. It's all here: the good, the bad, the beautiful and the ugly truths of life as he sees it.

Dr. Fred Gardaphé, Distinguished Professor
John D. Calandra, Italian American Institute
Queens College, CUNY
Author of *Moustache Pete is Dead*

Anyway, my hat is off to you, I love to write, but would never be able to put together anything like a book as you have. Kudos!

Loraine Kotary earned her Master's Degree in Secondary English Education from Syracuse University. She taught many years and recently returned as Associate Professor from State University of New York at Morrisville. She also spent many years as an adjunct of English Composition at Bryant and Stratton College.

Mario Fumarola's book is evocative of James Joyce's "stream of consciousness" style. His thoughts fly to the paper in a stream, clearly and succinctly as he experiences what he sees and feels. Thus, the reader gets a vivid picture of what Mario is seeing, as if we are following along with our video cameras recording all he sees, hears and feels.

As he writes, his love for the people he knew and the warmth that embraced him during his life is shared generously with his readers and audience.

Enjoy a spell of sitting on the porch and watching your neighbors go by or listening to the cacophonous sounds from the ethnically mixed neighborhoods of yesteryear—the feasts, the words—the simple faith—without pretension. His memories will become your memories.

Dr. Mary Custureri
Publisher Taylor and Seale Publishing, LLC.

Author : *Defy the Winds*
Strategies: Helping all Students Succeed
How to Learn in Ten Easy Steps
4 books of the *Happy Anderson Series*

Preface

How best to read *The Editor's Wastebasket*— Just Three Fleeting Thoughts………

The First Fleeting Thought

Have you ever skimmed a flat-faced pebble or small stone
across a quiet sleepy pond?
It will skip along happily…diving and climbing
across the surface of the pond…
making little splashes along the way to remind itself
(and you)
of where it has been, and where it is going.

The last splash, however brief and short lived disappears in
a microsecond, leaving ripples
that will not be there when you look again…
a splash that becomes the memory
of the flat faced stone,
the ripples which disappeared
become its tombstone.
The pebble will cease its merriment,
become submerged and drift lazily downward
to the bottom of the pond and await its eternity.

Some…maybe many…of the following stories will be
found to be light hearted, happy and carefree…
like a skipping stone over a pond surface,
but not all.
Here are some stories, like life itself,
that are sobering and thought provoking and sad… like a
submerged pebble
lying beneath the pond's surface.

The Second Fleeting Thought

Then there is the sound-bite concept. The book is very much like a collage: much to see, and the ensuing question, what is worth remembering and what is not?

The stories enclosed within will vary in topic and style of delivery. They may be humorous or sober. You may find the book compares with section D of your local daily newspaper, the section that includes comics and puzzles, arts and leisure, travel and food, life (personal features) and healthy living tips. The current and vital news is found in sections A, B, and C of the newspaper. Section D is more receptive to those seeking relaxation and those of us who are dreamers.

The Third Fleeting Thought

What, then, is the reader to expect? It is hoped: variety! Keep in mind, this is written by a well-qualified senior citizen, who has worn glasses for more than 65 years of his life and who has lost more footraces (and other races) than he thought humanly possible. He is accused of *selective hearing* by some, but remains fiercely proud of his Italian–American heritage.

He is just an old man standing with a cane and degenerate arthritis, looking back over a road traveled in eight decades, trying to focus with myopic vision and listening for the laughter of children.

Table of Contents

Acknowledgements

To Susan Loehr Wentzel, Allentown, PA and Charles R. Favreault Jr. Worcester, MA; you folks are great and you know as well as I do, that all this would never have come together without your help and understanding. My very sincere and heartfelt thanks.

Dr. Eugene P. Nassar and Robert Cimbalo, for your early encouragement that made me come to believe that I could be a storyteller. And Gino, your unwavering support. Your logical advice and your suggestions to me, were all God sent. And Bobby, you once told me that when someone starts to write in earnest, it (the writing) takes on a life of its own. You are a prophet.

Part I

Travel   Food

Pasta e Fagioli

A Coffee Shop on Bleecker Street

The Way of the Puglia

The Abbruzzi Connection

Pasta e Fagioli

We will call him Tony, but that is not his real name.

It wasn't 48 hours ago…after a day in St. Augustine…that Tony, his wife and another couple…stopped at an Italian restaurant on Route US 1 for dinner. In one of those heavy Florida downpours, this find turned out to be very fortunate….before and after dinner.

The owner's wife said they came from Calabria, and she spoke with a heavy and familiar accent. What pleased Tony more was that they used cloth napkins. Growing up, the families in the neighborhood called a napkin a *servettu,* and each person always had a cloth napkin for every meal. That was another time, maybe even another world.

After drinks and appetizers, the waitress dutifully announced the specials came with a salad or a soup, and the soup was *pasta e' fagioli.* Tony told the waitress that *pasta e' fagioli* was NOT a soup.

"Don't start!!!" Tony's wife hissed *sotto voce.* Predictably, he replied…for all to hear, "To me…it is a watered down bean soup…not *pasta e' fagioli!!!*"

Tony has his reasons.

When he was growing up in that three-story brownstone and in a cold water flat, Ma would make *pasta e' fagioli* for supper, and the second course was *pasta e' fagioli*. Ma made a kettle of it; you had a spoon and ate it from bowls (flat platters were for Sunday's pasta only). What we ate was not a soup; what we ate was meant to stick to your ribs.

There was always bread on the table, wine for Pa, water for the kids. The beans and tubini pasta were sprinkled with cheese. We ate with gusto, and we were content. The cheese would be freshly grated from a wedge that had black skin on the outside. The cheese wedge would be re-wrapped in butcher paper…which in time became oil stained…and returned to the ice-box (in years to come, the refrigerator). Ma would carefully 'bless' each of the bowls with a pinch of cheese…*come on Ma give me a little bit more!!!*

God bless Ma and Pa. There were always seconds.

AND…

The daily meals weren't just *pasta e' fagioli*. They could be *pasta e' piselli, pasta e' lenticchie, pasta e' ceci* Tony wondered why the restaurant industry didn't pursue liquifying pasta & peas…pasta & lentils…pasta & chick peas?   (Maybe *Progresso Soups* helped in developing the public image).

The kids reminded each other that Sunday was a macaroni day, and Ma always made a big bowl of meatballs and sometimes spareribs (pick the rib clean and gnaw at the bone tasting the saucy marrow).   *Maybe Pa will buy a chicken from Patsy the Chicken Man this Saturday I am gunna get a drumstick this time!!!*

That was another time…maybe another world.
The owners may have come from Calabria and the cute waitress might well be American Italian-Irish, and Tony knows it is **their time** and not his. But..**in that other time**, *pasta e' fagioli* was not a soup, nor was it a substitute for salad, but the first and last course. BUT….thank God…it wasn't *la miseria* either.

Tony half smirked to himself as he thought, "Ma and Pa's *miseria* was not like his or that of his generation, (there was actual hunger back then), nor any more than his *miseria* was what his own kids experienced…and thank God, his grandkids will never know or feel the physical and mental anguish of *la miseria!!!*"

He laughed aloud when he realized, in a decade… maybe a decade and a half….who in the hell is going to know or care if *pasta e' fagioli* was a soup or a………

It'll be someone else's time.

A Coffee Shop on Bleecker Street

We will call him Tony. That is not his real name, but it fits the character and this narrative. Tony grew up in East Utica, the very lower East Side. Today, in a suburban town very far away, Tony really enjoys his retirement, his wine and his stogie, and in his quiet moments can quickly scroll back up to his past *"in the blink of a young girl's eye"* (lyrics from a Springsteen song). He (like you) can do it as easily as if he was touching a *pg up or pg dn* (page up or page down) key on his computer. Occasionally, he finds himself physically back there, but, like his wife and kids, they are no longer **there.** He now lives far away…far away from the city of his youth…and far from that special time… and that special way of life. But the French say. *the more things change…the more they stay the same.*

Tony's wife's uncle passed away. *Yes…of course… we'll go…we gotta go!!!* He always liked Uncle Bill; he was a good guy. They (especially Tony) have been back numerous times in the past, and Tony was well aware of the creeping blight that so many old cities in the Northeast have and are experiencing. It just happens…change…the suburban flight…shopping malls…two-stall garages… Little League…soccer moms…Grammies with grey Cadillac's…new churches that look more like concert halls or auditoriums than churches. *Where are the Stations of the Cross…oh, over there??? Ya sure??? Dey don't look like the stations we had at St. Anthony's.*

Ah..!!! but the more things change… the more they stay the same…??

There were three coffee shops on Bleecker Street when Tony was growing up. They were named; The Mellow Shop, The Goody Shop and Whitey's (the cop) Lunch. If you wanted, you could say that all three where bracketed inside the two predominant Catholic Churches of East Utica, St. Anthony of Padua, anchoring the far east, and Our Lady of Mt. Carmel, a western pillar… like the one in Brindisi signifying the end of the Appian Way… marking the far west.

And within these yet beautiful and still-existing landmarks, was a magical world that today only old senior citizens seem to want to remember. Aah!!! but it was complete and vibrant and noisy and full of life…a push cart with an old woman that smoked DeNapoli Tuscany cigars…lemonade trucks or carts that sold a cone of lemon ice for 3 cents and another for five cents…a push cart with its bed filled with chopped ice, offering clams on the half shell every Saturday starting at noon…closing when sold out. They called the hawker "The Hindu" ("only a nickel each… not many left"). Who can remember? But Tony can.

He vaguely remembers the trolleys on Bleecker Street and with clarity those big lumbering yellow and orange buses that replaced them…he knew…and he just remembers all.

Vacant lots now dominate the area where tenement houses were and police call boxes were mounted on telephone poles…and pool rooms and drug stores…butcher shops…grocery stores…shoe-repair shops…barber shop. All thrived, and all serviced a Mediterranean-immigrant population. Mediterranean because there were pockets of Lebanese and Syrian families, (those kids, we used to call Turks).

So much of it has disappeared in the foggy smoke of time. The wretched few structures that remain stand as beaten and weary warriors among the fallen…those that fell into disuse and deterioration and eventually, the death of demolition.

The Mellow Shop guys, mostly Sicilians, all belonged to Mt. Carmel. The Goody Shop boys were either St. Anthony's or Mt. Carmel's, because it was Kossuth Avenue that divided the two parishes. The Goody Shop was right around the corner from Kossuth on Bleecker. Whitey's was strictly all St. Anthony's guys.

The Goody Shop boys and the guys from Whitey's were mostly Barese and Calabrian or Bruzzese. You can see St. Anthony's from the back door of Whitey's, and from the Mellow Shop…right around the corner from Mohawk… and up on the fourth floor…from De Rosa's Hall…you could look over the rooftops and see the back of Our Lady of Mt. Carmel Church. With a good ear and a good sense of direction, you could hear the peals of the church bells from in front of the Goody Shop.

Whitey's (the cop) Lunch is the only one left.

Tony and his wife were to attend the funeral mass and the internment of Uncle Bill. They had to be at the funeral home by 9:45. The mass was at ten-thirty, internment after Mass and a luncheon at the Monarch Restaurant…way over on the west side. He sort of suggested breakfast at Whitey's in lieu of the motel restaurant for two reasons. The first, because he himself wanted to stop by and see if any of the boys were around… sometimes they'd meet there before going golfing, and the second, he wanted to give Chris (the owner for the past thirty five years) something.

He approached the subject gingerly for several reasons, not the least of which was he was wondering how his wife would accept the ambiance and the condition of the luncheonette. You see, like Tony and East Utica, Whitey's was showing signs of old age: old booths along the wall…an open kitchen behind the ten stool counter… tables in the rear with non-matching chairs…linoleum tile floor…old fashion coat hangers…posters (mostly New York Yankees) on the wall…above the cashier a sign reading…*If you need credit go to Helen Waite*…smart-alecky waitress…and most of all…big Chris in front of his grill…working, talking, tight high white apron...like a cummerbund…horn rim glasses…thick arms and shoulders…booming voice…talking about yesterday's game…stepping to the 'piano' when a customer was ready to go…all that…and more…*How is his wife going to take it???*

Tony need not have fretted…his Polish-American wife saw all the beauty of the spectacle…all of it!!! *Next time we come to Utica, we'll come here for breakfast!!! His pepper, eggs and cheese omelet is to die for…they pre-cook the peppers and it softens them up…it was good!!!*

Hey Tony how you doin??? When didja get in???

I got sumptin for ya...

At Whitey's Lunch on Bleecker Street, you will not find matching coffee cups and saucers. Instead, you will be served a promotional mug from somewhere or other...a bank opening...American Red Cross...Vito's fine sausage....Aetna Life and Health...and it goes on.

Yeah??? What???...

I got this..."

What izit???

Open it and see fur-yer-self...

Chris opened the square cardboard box and said ... *Hey all right!!!...I always can use 'em!!!*

I know, you cheap bastard...you could try buying cups and saucers instead of scrounging 'em once in a while... The promotional coffee mug...maroon in color with silver lettering read: Italian-Americans Read *Primo Magazine*.

Hey tanks...but I gunna charge ya for breakfast anyway...

Yeah...everybody knows you throw nickels around like manhole covers (Tony read that once in a book).

Chris closes at two and is off Sundays. It is convenient for him to have free afternoons; he umpires local high school, American Legion, and college baseball games. He loves and knows the game. His physical width more so than his height, his (when necessary) booming voice and his thick skin are all good attributes for this part-time endeavors.

Tony stepped up to the glass counter with the local and NYC newspapers at the corner, and waited for Chris to come so he could pay up. Chris wiped his hands and as he approached asked…*How was it?? Everything okay???*

"*Yeah*, sure, the wife loved it."

Hey tanks for the mug.

"Sure, I got more than enough at home." Tony paid and left his tip with Chris to give to the waitresses.

Well see ya next time…

"You got it…Hey Chris you gotta do me a favor"

Yeah sure, what???…

"You really got to quit cutting your own hair…that is the worse haircut I saw all year…go to a barber, will ya? They all laughed and Tony and his wife left.

A lotta guys from East Utica…the Goody Shop boys, Whitey's gang, and the Mellow Shop guys…possess this…(what is it)…moxie toughness…quick wittiness…

brash boldness…opinionated self confidence…whatever…
The boys from Bleecker Street recognize and practice it.

The more things change…the more they stay the same.

We will call him Tony, but that is not his real name…

On his last trip up to Utica and since he got there about noon, Tony made the usual afternoon rounds…Joey's for lunch, then down to 900 block of Bleecker to see Big John at his used furniture store…and the parade of humanity that crosses his threshold and…then down to the VFW…for a couple with Big John and whoever follows him out…and then to the apartments and then to the PFC dinner…back to the Sons of Italy Hall…where in Tony's opinion he belonged.

Things do change and they don't…Tony remembers that Chris took over Whitey's (the cop) Lunch when he was just nineteen. Chris had a bout with cancer and his sons tried to run the luncheonette, and it was eventually sold. It has changed ownership several times. The last time Tony saw the luncheonette, it was closed and had a For Sale sign in the window.

The Way of the Puglia

We'll call him Tony, but that is not his real name, it just makes it easier for him to tell the story. Yes, he was sure it was the philosopher, George Santayana, who said something like "Those who do not learn from history are forced to relive it."

Tony's paternal grandfather was born April 12th, 1849 in a small village called Cisternino in the then Bourdon dominated Kingdom of Naples. Today, the village's name remains unchanged, but it is now mapped in the Provence of Brindisi, Italia in the fertile Apuglia region. Twisted and very, very old olive tree groves abound in the Puglia; with their small green-gray leaves showing you two faces when the wind blows even just a little bit. In the fall the farmers have to prop up the tree branches with boards and long thick broken branches to help support the additional weight of the olives. Seeing an olive tree for the first time, a body could easily think that their trunks were just huge pieces of driftwood haphazardly stuck in the ground by a wrathful Mother Nature.

The fertile soil in most of the region has a distinct reddish-brown hue.

The fields also teem with many fieldstones... sometimes flashing dirty grayish white against the reddish brown soil. In time they too were put to good use, making stone fences and the unique coned shaped roofs of the trulli. The stone trulli, and the stone wall fences, grew old with the bountiful olive groves. All this time — weary ugliness or beauty, because both are in the eyes of the beholder — adds greatly to the panorama fantasy…the beauty and serenity of the countryside. On clear days you can see the Adriatic Sea from the heights.

About three thousand miles due west, there are no olive trees where Tony lives in Pennsylvania; the closest he comes to Mediterranean husbandry are a few fragile fig trees. They are very sensitive, susceptible to vermin and freezing cold, it remains an annual challenge to keep the fig trees alive. In comparison, a fig tree is a flash in the pan to one of those majestic olive trees in Apuglia, but that is there and he is here in the United States.

Last month he attended the monthly 'PFC' get together dinner at the old Sons of Italy in Utica. PFC stands for Proctor Fifties Club: Proctor being his old high school. After any one of those buffet dinners, the guys would cluster in groups at various tables…batting the breeze… drinking some wine or beer, some even sipping grappa… and if you were lucky, you'll find yourself with some pretty well-read old timers who thrive on Roman history. As was the case at this meeting.

*Did you know the Romans built a bridge over the
Rhine in just ten days?*
*Did you know the Appian Way starts in Rome and
ends in Brindisi and they built an obelisk that still stands
today???*
*Did you know when the Romans destroyed
Carthage, their Legions killed 100,000 Carthaginians with
their broad short swords???*

Did you know that war started because the Carthaginians destroyed olive trees in Italy?

How could olive groves be the cause of so much bloodshed?

Who would believe that the old tired and twisted olive tree with her small pointed leaves that show you another shade of dusty gray-green when there is even the slightest breeze…that warm sticky August breeze from the Sahara Desert called the Sirocco…who would know that in time the olive tree branch would come to symbolize peace? Carthage was brutally destroyed.

When he and his wife visited Cisternino in 2007, one of his distant cousins… and through marriage at that… Pino gave him an insight into the depth of the male mentality in the Puglia. He had once seen on PBS television, a documentary documenting the life of Greek fishermen fishing the coastal waters. Like Pino does at least once a week in his blue Adriatic Sea, the televised Greeks were fishing for octopus. Then Tony recalled the narrator of the documentary telling and showing how the Greeks would bait and lure the octopus to the surface and adroitly net or snag them. Once on board the small open boat, the fisherman picks up the wiggling octopus and bites the back of its neck to kill him. The narrator went on to explain… death is instantaneous for the octopus and this was the most humane way to do it. (What else would you expect from a public correct broadcasting system?)

Pino and his friends use the same method.

Pino is one sharp cookie. His father was killed on board an Italian submarine after an aerial attack by the RAF late in the Second World War, and he himself entered a maritime academy. However, he was forced to drop out because of digestive problems. He was an only child, and his mother remained widowed until her death. He eloped with Tony's cousin and went to work for the postal system way '*up in Milan.*' About 1976 or 77, he, his wife and two daughters returned to Cisternino. They soon had their first and only son and promptly named him after his hero grandfather Fabbio, who had died aboard a submarine.

Pino always maintained an academic curiosity, constantly reading, asking questions and remaining politically knowledgeable. In Italy, that is quite an accomplishment. Pino once told him that not so long ago, if a man willfully and deliberately destroyed one of your olive trees, it was considered 'justifiable homicide' for you to kill him. Olive trees can easily live a couple of hundred years, and if you were to plant an olive tree from seeds at age thirty, it is very unlikely you'll live to see its full potential.

They...those from the Pulglia...take their olive trees quite seriously.

Tony was sort of shocked upon hearing of such quick and decisive punishment on the part of the injured party. His lifelong Puglia host replied,"*What did the American do with horse and cattle thieves in your Old West?*"

Neither of Tony's paternal grandparents was literate, nor did they ever come to America, and neither ever traveled more than sixty miles (as the crow flies) from Cisternino: to either Taranto or Brindisi. Other than an old framed, horizontal, glass protected oval postcard size photograph, Tony and his brothers had never seen them. His mother would have him and his brothers kiss the cool glass that protected the picture every Sunday after Mass (for a while anyway). It was done to show respect and honor to our *genitori.*

When Tony was growing up, his Ma would tell stories of what she saw and of what she was told about Cisternino. Back then, in the late nineteen-twenties, Tony's aunts played matchmaker—little Italian yentas who had an unwed sister back in the old country.

Koomba Pietro (he was a koomba because he baptized Aunt Grace's Antoinette*) when you go back to visit your mother and father, you should visit our family in Vasto,....you'd be doing us all a service if you could deliver this hundred dollars to my father and Maria Nicola our eldest sister. She has a family of her own but they all live together...my father and our two sisters...ever since our mother died in 1917. One of my sisters is only twenty one. She is healthy and smart...she can cook...she can read and sew...she learned a lot at the convent...you should be thinking of raising a family. You don't want to be a boarder forever unless you are a priest. You are strong and healthy. Don't you want a family?*

Tony's father went to Santo Ferrera, the local ticket agent, to book passage for his return trip to Italy. It had been six years since he first came to America. He was an American *cittadino* (citizen). In September of that year,

Aunt Lucy had her sixth child, another daughter making five girls and only one son…for now. They named the baby Carmella, and Tony's father baptized her just before he left for six months. Till the day he died, most of his older American nieces called him Koomba Pete, in lieu of Uncle Pete. Godfather or Uncle is a name or title of respect and he, Tony's father, never had any preference.

As a kid, Tony would love to listen to his mother talk about the four or five weeks she spent in Cisternino. She had married his father on April 12th, 1928. They were wed in her hometown in the Province of Abruzzi called Vasto. His father's parents did not attend the wedding. In their stead, he brought along his eldest 14 year old niece, because…as Tony's Ma told him…his family had to be represented. Plus, the young girl would be good company for her and an excellent liaison in those first awkward moments in any marriage. Over the years, this little act of mutual protection and bonding blossomed into a genuine loving friendship.

Tony's Mom told him that his grandfather would drink coffee in the morning and his grandmother preferred vino cotto (cooked wine). His grandfather reprimanded his father once for taking Ma out to the fields to dig potatoes because she was…"*a small fragile city girl who could read and write and sing like a bird!!!*"

Ma told Tony about living in a *trulli* and making the bed. The bed was bigger and higher than what she was used to, the room was cramped, and she had to take off her shoes and walk on the bed to straighten out the far corners, then tug the blankets taunt. His grandfather was a big man, and once one of the pigs escaped from the sty and damaged some of his grape vines. His grandfather cursed at the runaway pig and vowed he'd *"kill you* (him) *with my bare hands."* The animal was recaptured and Ma told Tony, his grandmother pleaded with his grandfather to let it live until the fall when they normally slaughtered. It was not to be. Olive trees or grape vines are to be protected, and failing that, avenged.

Tony's mom went on to tell that this angry avenger had been married twice. His first wife died after only three months of marriage. He courted and wed his second wife, nee Vita Magolino. However, prior to the marital union that lasted much more than a half-century, there were obstacles. Vita's older brothers violently protested, even to the point of beating her because they were so sure that if she married this young widower, she, too, would soon die. Little Tony's eyebrows arched upward and his eyes bulged as he asked, *"Why Ma...why would they beat their own sister???"*

Tony, just a kid at the time...maybe first grade or kindergarten, clearly remembered his mother's response, ..."*Eeh...it was different in those days...the contadini (farmers) were ignorant and superstitious. They were not educated...don't be hard on them. Their acts were foolish, but they loved their sister...and believed they were only protecting her."* Tony's grandfather proved to be a good worker, a good provider and most of all a good husband.

> ***Such were and are the men of the Puglia...***
> ***and their families...***
> ***and their lives...***
> ***and their fig trees...***
> ***and their olive trees.***

The Abbruzzi Connection

Tony's maternal grandfather was born July 20th, 1860 in the French-dominated Kingdom of Naples, the year before the unification of Italy. Today, the village's name remains unchanged, but it is now mapped in the Providence of Abruzzi, Vasto, in the county seat of Chieti, Italia. The last time Tony was there, archaeologists were excavating both Greek and Roman ceramic floor tiles. Tony was told by the archeologist they could distinguish them from one another simply because the Greeks worked with black and white tiles and the Romans used multicolored pieces.

On one of his earlier visits, he was informed that at one time Vasto, was called Hostruim, and it actually pre-dates Rome. The sea-faring Philistines, Greeks, Turks and Arabs all conducted business at this Adriatic village high up in the mountains overlooking the beautiful blue sea. The villagers raised sheep and bartered wool and salted meat with sea-going foreigners.

The old village had, a long time ago, built a wall or fort for protection against pirates and raiders. Portions of the wall still remain in the center of the town. What makes these ruins unique is that parts of the remaining wall tell us it was in the shape of a vessel, with a bow and circular conning tower like the raised platform on a ship.

The Romans also left evidence of their stay — ask any young urchin to show *La Porta Vecchia* or *La Porta Nuova*. Close by, in the town square, stands a monument to one of its favorite sons, Gabriele Rossetti. It seems that everyone who visits Vasto, must see and take photographs of the monument, the high walled bow of the fortress and the old Roman gates of the town.

Tony and his wife once stood near a three foot stone fence overlooking the panorama of the Adriatic so far down below. It was breathtaking, and remains so till this day. His wife wondered out loud why anyone would want to leave such a heavenly place. Tony knew, and he could answer it in a word: *la miseria.* He had heard it so often growing up.

Ma told Toni her father was not an attractive man being somewhat short and further cursed with a hunched back, especially noticeable with advancing age. In wide eyed wonderment, Tony listened as Ma went on to say that her father, with the help of a brother, kidnapped his grandmother and then ran off into the interior. Her mother had been only fourteen years old then. The brazen act (according to Ma) was neither lustful nor for carnal knowledge: Grandpa meant the girl no harm, but he needed a wife.

When they eventually returned to their village, the shameful bold act of this short hunched-back man could only be pardoned by the citizenry and the Holy Mother Church by a marriage. Hence, nee Surianni Anna Francesca became, in the eyes of the citizenry and in the eyes of God, Tony's grandmother. They were married for thirty-five years, had ten children, and sometimes had dreams of coming to America.

Over the years of hearing hundreds of stories about the 'old country,' Tony came to sense his grandmother was not very happy with her life. Surprisingly (to Tony, anyway), she was fiercely protective and loving to her children—like a grizzly bear protecting her cubs, but inevitably when the time came, abandoning them. Ma once told Tony, she was beaten by her mother when she didn't want her hair brushed out. Another time Ma, who always suffered from bad feet, found that her mother had cut the sides of her shoes to ease the pressure on her 'corns.'

Tony's Uncle Pietro was beaten by Tony's grandmother when a few days before his wedding date he announced he did not wish to be married. To hear Ma tell it, he was literally beaten into submission. He was twenty three years old.

Ma would tell Tony that when she was a little girl, in the evening her mother and youngest daughter would go to the outskirts of the town to dispose of the bodily wastes accumulated during the day. On the way back home, they would stop at a little chapel called *La Madonna della Catena* (Our Lady of the Chain). They would kneel and start to say the Rosary for the family members in America. The little one would eventually lie down on the cool stones of the opened shrine to watch the fire-flies and then would fall asleep. Her mother would finish the five mysteries of the Rosary, pick up the little girl and carry her back up the hill to her bed.

Back in 1913, Tony's grandfather, his second eldest daughter Carmella, and his fourth son, Vincenzo, came to America. They were met in New York by his eldest son, Joseph, who had come to America eight years earlier in 1905. Tony remembers being told two different stories about what happened to his grandfather at Ellis Island. The first was that he did not pass the eye examination; the other was that there was a bureaucratic mix-up in the paper work. Whatever the reason, he was returned to Italy alone, leaving Carmella and Vincenzo in the care of his eldest son, Joseph. Tony often wondered if the rejection might have been because of his crooked back.

By 1915, Ma had two brothers and a sister living in America. On March 14th 1915, her brother Vincent died of tuberculosis. He was not quite nineteen years old. Tony's aunts and uncles and his mom agree in unison that when the news finally arrived, it sounded the death toll for his grandmother. Shortly thereafter, she, too, passed, lamenting to her last day that she should not have given her blessing to her son Vincent to come to America. As the fates would have it, her husband was not at home when she died. He was working as an itinerant laborer in the South, harvesting olives in Apuglia.

As World War I was ending, a tired, bent old man that may have drunk a little too much wine, found work as a gardener, orderly, and caretaker at the only hospital in Vasto. After the death of his wife and his return from Apuglia, he and his family merged with his recently married eldest daughter, Maria Nicola. According to Ma, hard times followed.

One day, maybe in early July or August of 1927, a letter came from America. Maria Nicola, the eldest daughter, so very bright and intelligent the nuns at the convent thought she should become a teacher, read it aloud to the extended family—now numbering her husband, five daughters and four sons, her two sisters and TaTa in a four room apartment. *Yes everyone is well and all trying to prosper...Michael isn't married yet...but is seeing two different girls, one of which is Irish. Lucia is pregnant (again) and expecting in September...that'll make five. Giuseppi's wife has had two still-born since their marriage in 1916...and are resolved that God wishes them to be 'grandfather and grandmother' to their American nieces and nephews. He is negotiating to buy the Ritrona Bakery on Morehead Street.*

And the letter went on to inform them...*They have a boarder, a Barese who was returning to visit his elderly parents in Apuglia for at least six months. He is an American cittadino (*an American citizen) *and will return. He is an honorable and respected man who incidentally stood Godfather to my little Donetta, and Lucia has already asked that he stand Godfather to her new baby. In the summer, he works pouring and floating concrete roads all over the countryside, and in the winter works occasionally in the textile mills. He can read and write...like our Chiara. We have asked him to stop by and visit Papa when he comes to Italy.*

Ma told Tony Pa wrote to her father shortly after arriving in November and visited Vasto before Christmas for two days. Pa had delivered an envelope from her siblings to her father. He was very grateful because at times in the past, the postal systems didn't deliver. No one was sure as to what side of the Atlantic the 'loss' occurred. Ma said her father told her it was her decision. If she approved of him and wanted to go to America (some of her brothers and sisters were there), she had his blessing.

Funny thing, Ma also told Tony that prior to the visit from the Barese, she was contemplating becoming a nun. The newly-acquainted corresponded for a few months, and in April of 1928, accompanied by his 15 year old niece, Pa went back to Vasto. On the eve of her wedding day, the twelfth of April, Ma and the fifteen year old future niece went to the little chapel-shrine of the Madonna of the Chain and replaced the Altar linen. She had done the fringe embodiment shortly after she met Pa. And another funny thing, Tony never asked her why, although maybe it is for the best.

To get to Saint Anthony of Padua Church in Utica, New York, from Tony's five room apartment in the brownstone, you walked east on Catherine for six city blocks. On the second block, there was a one-family frame dwelling where one of the very few old German families resided. The owners prided themselves for the rose bushes they grew. Their front yard was really a touch of heaven and color in the old neighborhood. Ma would go to mass every morning, and on her way home one bright and early July day, she paused—no,… stopped—for the longest time and just admired the beautiful rose bushes. The owner stepped onto his front porch and they nodded hello, and then Ma said she had hoped he didn't mind, but she was just admiring his beautiful roses and added that her father could grow roses like that in the front of the hospital in the *Old Country*. The owner beamed with pride, told her to wait a second, went into the house and returned with shears. He cut the most beautiful rose and gave it to Ma.

She could not have been any happier if he had given her a sack of gold. She slowly walked back to the brownstone, down the alley and up the rear staircase. When she entered the five room flat, she quietly wept as she remembered...*a tired, bent old man who may have drunk a little too much wine, that found work as a gardener, orderly and caretaker at the only hospital in Vasto.* He wanted to come to America because he felt he could do better for his family and for those he loved and those that loved him.

Part II

Human Interest & Life

A Better Man Than I

Smiles

Good Old Walter
Whadda Ya Do with Old Baggage
Something to Be Said
It Is Those Small Things

How to Build a Rectory

The Pear Tree

The Loyal Sons

The Glorious Summer and Fall of 1945

A Better Man Than I

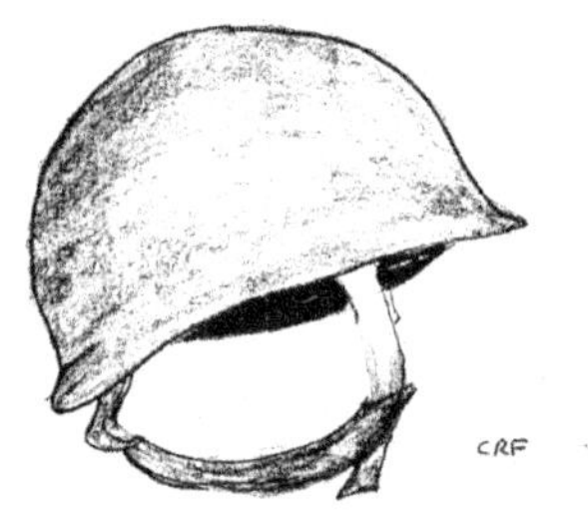

Tony said to himself, "I guess it all started out simple enough. Just two eighty-year-old guys (*old army buddies*) recalling their basic training days at Fort Riley, Kansas." Tony reluctantly admitted that it was a long lifetime ago…way back in the summer of 1957.

Today their 'memory exchanges', with the wonders of modern technology, are done electronically, and they run the gamut of various topics and incidents. "Remember? Rim Rock Ridge with the big Blue Spade painted onto that enormous slab of concrete...up there near the top? How 'bout Sergeant Ramo? (He *had that thick Puerto Rican accent.) H*ow 'bout the Post Exchange (PX)? with their three-point-two beer? Remember the fist fight in the barracks between Fleming and French? The rifle range? Where Charlie qualified as a sharpshooter and Tony just eked out 143 to qualify—*funny how you remember something as insignificant as that*—and a zillion other stories. But the one recollection that puts Tony on the top edge of a dark bottomless abyss, and helplessly wrapped in his vertigo phobia—was the recollection of the infiltration course.

AAH…the infiltration course!

In the twilight of his life, reflecting on his past sins (which may never be absolved), to the very few decent things he accomplished—life (selfishness versus charity—giving or taking) and inevitability death, becomes very complicated as he stands on and at the abyss's rim. The baggage he is carrying can become very troublesome. But Tony knows of just one man who, if there is to be a life after, is certain to be standing in the light because of an act of kindness that was never forgotten by the recipient. It happened at the infiltration course.

Tony was inducted into the Army June 21st, 1957, was processed at Fort Dix, New Jersey along with inductees from the Northeast and sent to Fort Riley, Kansas, arriving there on July 1st. The recruits merged with others from the Midwest and Southeast (*slower lower*) and all of them assigned to the 26th Infantry Regiment for basic training—specifically, Company A, Second Platoon. First squad, Staff Sergeant Sigmund Ramos platoon leader.

Tony recalled their last muster at Fort Dix and some future *wanna be staff sergeant and probably standup comedian* having a captive audience, addressed the anxious recruits with duffle bags packed and written orders in hand awaiting transportation:

Sooo you guys are going to Kansas Huh?

Ah yeah…Kansas…..

The only place in the whole world where you can stand in six inches of mud and watch a dust storm...

Oh   yeah! Kansas...the only thing between the North Pole and Kansas was an old beat up barbed wire fence...and that darn thing blew over last year and it is lying flat now.

There were the expected chuckles and smirks...and secretly...a little anxiety, but later both Tony and Charlie agreed that NCO may have been a prophet. In those twenty or so weeks he spent in Kansas, Tony was the hottest he has ever been, and once in December (during Advance Infantry Training) he has never been colder, waiting for transportation back to the barracks after a three day field bivouac.

Company A was scheduled to go first to the infiltration course, at 0700 hours, but due to a glitch, the motor pool did not get the duces'n'half out to the company area until nearly ten. That August day broke clear and hot, and those waiting for transportation on the parade grounds became very wearisome. They were marched to the parade grounds shortly after breakfast in full gear (back pack, cartridge belt with accessories attached, steel pot and weapon) and waited. And, so typical of military service, they had hurried up to wait.

There was a something about Charlie (Tony's buddy) that made Tony often think that Charlie must have read every book ever printed. And it was through Charlie that Tony 'learned' that Kipling's "Gunga Din" was not a book but a poem. That is what Hollywood can do.

Transportation finally arrived, and all the men of Company A piled in. The infiltration course was much further away than any of them anticipated, and they were all grateful that they didn't have to march to the site. The course itself had not been used in years. It remained in a state of disrepair in spite of the fact an ordnance/engineer detail spent two days prepping the area and setting charges. They also did string out more barbed wire & unrolled concertina wire.

The trucks rumbled and bounced and pitched and yawn to the course, which should have made for refreshing air movement, but really did not. It was just one of those days; like standing in the mud and watching a dust storm and getting hotter by the minute. If truth be known, of the two-hundred or so canteens attached to waists of the men, who were now unloading from the trucks and getting into formation, fifty percent were already drained empty and the other fifty percent had no more than half a cup of water remaining, if that.

First and Second Platoon, fall on your Guide ons...Third and Fourth Platoons stand fast...

The course was framed by a long u-shaped trench. The two platoons marched single file down each of the sides and met in the center of the lateral trench. The lateral pit had a 'step cut' its entire length and was to be used as a firing step or, as was the case this date, a step to get you up and over the top. From the step the men saw two machine gun bunkers, about twenty yards apart, and ten yards from the perimeter. They saw the wire fences and the concertina. The pit sergeants verified each man had minimum combat gear: steel pot, bayonet and cartridge belt with canteen.

Before stepping onto the step cut, they were ordered to fix bayonets. The first run was a dry run; other than the heat, it was uneventful and took about fifteen minutes to complete. When they reached the gun pits, they all tumbled and or eased into still another safety trench, caught their breaths, returned their bayonets to the scabbards and were ordered to scramble out. The midday heat, the annoyance of wearing the heavy steel pot, and the sweat and dirt accumulated during the run was starting to take a heavier toll.

They returned to the step cuts and prepared for the 'wet run' and the introduction to live ammo being fired overhead *(...dat ought to be nuff to keep your head down...)*.

The first and second squad lined up on the jump-off step...almost shoulder to shoulder...the third and fourth squad stood in the deeper trench awaiting their turn. The pit sergeant constantly yelled and repeated instructions. *"Belly-button or asshole to the ground at ALL TIMES. Do not get tangled in the barbed wire. Spread out...stay within markers...you cluster they'll set off a charge...keep moving...belly button and assholes....spread out...keep moving. If you got to twist onto your back to get under and past a wire, keep the rifle between you and the wire... don't get tangled up...*

Tony and most of the other guys had their M-1 rifles on the lip of the trench; he noticed one of the pit sergeants raise an eight foot wooden flag pole with an eighteen inch green circular tin on top. Then they hear whistles blow and *Go!!! Go!!! Go!!!*

They moved out...staying on their backs or stomachs...like snakes. They moved forward using their knees (scissors-like) and when on their backs, pushing hard directly on the back heel of their boots.

They heard the thirty caliber guns firing, and they heard the bullets whistle more distinctly overhead, and still others thought they saw a tracer round here and there. They continued to move. Moving under low hanging barbed wire, they twisted over onto their backs, placed the rifle on their stomach and faces. As they inched forward, they raised the wire away from themselves.

Safely passing under one such wire, Tony flopped over onto his stomach again, giving himself a much better view. He quickly evaluated how much more there was to go. Happily he could see the bottom of the gun emplacement and safety trench beneath it. Twenty-five yards to go!!! He reached back, got just a *little bit more...* and started to move a little faster.

Then it happened. The guns stopped firing. A siren went off...wailing its mournful cry. The pit-sergeants' whistles all started to blow in unison. A First Lieutenant in one of the gun bunkers was yelling *cease fire, cease fire* into the squawk box. Then another audible instruction. A second later, *stay down!!! Stay down! Nobody move! Keep those assholes or belly buttons on the ground!*

Soon some of those lying in the now very still and quite barbed wire field began to feel the resurgence of the sun's mid-day heat. Tony tipped his steel pot so that the rim rested on his nose, giving just an iota of comfort. The talk picked up among the postulated men. News flashes crisscrossed the barbed wire field.

Short round…somebody got shot in the buttocks.

Guy was in the second wave….fourth Squad…

Not in the ass…he caught it in the back…spinal column…medics are there

They are moving up the ambulance

He's gotta go to the Main Post Hospital…

Tony was starting to breathe very heavily now. His body produced another surge of sweat. His fatigue blouse was soaked, and the front and back of his trousers were soaked through.

I'm sorry for the guy who got shot…I hope he makes it…but please God…Please!!! Get me out of here!!!

A century later, they all heard the officer announce over the squawk box, *Evacuation complete…stand by to open fire…pit sergeants are they ready to move?*

A pause...*Open Fire!!!* Like a bunch of muddy and dirty worms, 'A' Company crawled forward.

When Tony reached the safety trench, he did a three to nine from a twelve to six, dropping his right arm over the lip of the trench. Bracing himself, he gave one last scissor kick and tumbled into the trench. He collected himself somewhat, took an inventory...steel pot...rifle...cartridge belt...canteen...and then rested his back on the vertical wall of the trench. He knew he had to stand...the quicker the better...or these guys would be dropping on him.

Charlie tumbled into the trench, and a second later was followed by Ginsberg, (who had a nasty gash on his right shoulder). Both decided to remain seated for a while. All of them were exhausted, overheated, and thirsty.

Then Dolan, one of the biggest guys in the Company, fell into the trench right beside Tony. He, too, was not only very exhausted...overheated, and tired, but insanely angry from lack of water. "You got any water in your canteen?" he asked Tony.
Tony was picking off globs of mud paddies from his fatigues like the portions of pancakes you leave on a breakfast plate, and maybe not in the most sympathetic mood he replied to the very angry Irish-American, "Not a drop. Used it all to wash my Rolls Royce this morning!" His sarcasm or wit earned him nothing but a half shove and a dirty look.

Dolan then went to Ginsberg lying down half conscious and very immobile. Ginsberg just shook his head *No!*

Dolan then spotted Charlie who, seated, with his back leaning against the trench wall, and with maybe a cup of water in his canteen, had been watching the big guy's search for water. Willing to share half his water, Charlie took his canteen off his cartridge belt, and began unscrewing its cap.

"Let me take a swig and you can have this." He made a very noble gesture that fell upon deaf ears. Dolan was over him, reaching down to grab the canteen out of Charlie's hand…Charlie tightened his grip, but Dolan literally lifted Charlie off the ground, twisted his shoulder into Charlie's chest, and wrenched the canteen from his hands. He began to inhale the entire contents of the canteen while Charlie was flailing with his arms as much as he could to no avail.

From the gun pits above, the Lieutenant yelled down, "What the hell is going on down there?"

Nuttin!!! It is all under control…we are squared away down here…no problem." was the chorus's answer.

The trench was becoming very crowded and busy. Tony remembered where the staging area was when Company A got off of the trucks. It was over in that direction, and he remembered a tree line. *I could enjoy shade as much as a canteen of water.* Noticing a wooden ladder between the gun pits, he shouldered his rifle and walked to the shadows of a tree line.

Tony made his way to the staging area and as he approached it he noticed a soldier standing guard over the entire area. His vantage point was under the tree branches. He was black, and maybe even though not being as tall or wide as Tony, he looked formidable enough.

"I am with Company A, Second Platoon. My gear is right here." As Tony pointed to a row of similar equipment…back pack…gas mask…poncho, he showed the sentinel the last four digits of his serial number stenciled onto some of his gear. They nodded their agreement in unison, and Tony laid his steel pot and cartridge belt onto the pile. He said to the guard, "I'm going to suck up some of your shade. I've never been this hot."

Tony sat with his back against a maple tree and exercised his neck muscles, happy to be rid of the heavy metal helmet. It felt so good. Their eyes met, and Tony asked…almost half heartedly., "Do you have any water?"

The kid looked him squarely in the eyes, but did not respond. He merely twisted to the side and took his canteen off his belt. Tony was on his feet, standing right beside him by the time the canteen was off his belt. Tony kept his hands at his side, almost holding his breath, and reached for it when it was silently offered. He took a mouth full of water, but he did not swallow right away. He closed his eyes and swirled the water around in his mouth; then he swallowed and opened his eyes.

He studied the face of his black Aquarius, brown eyes, his nostrils, his thick lips…and then he started to hand him the canteen back, but stopped. In a mid-air gesture, Tony lightly bounced the canteen, like asking permission to drink again. His name was Stankey, and Stankey nodded 'yes.'

Rudyard Kipling opens the poem "Gunga Din" with the lines:

You may talk o' gin and beer
When you're quartered safe out 'ere

And he closes with

Though I've belted you and flayed you,
By the livin' Gawd that made you
You're a better man than I am, Gunga Din!

Dolan, Ginsberg, Charlie and Tony were all indeed eventually satisfied. If truth be known, it was Dolan who ordered the first pitcher of beer that very night at the Regimental Post Exchange. And rest assured in time… and...*quartered safe out here* …they all partook in liquid satisfaction in Kansas and numerous guest houses in Germany.

There was an incident a long time ago, in a place where you could watch a dust storm and be standing in six inches of mud that Tony remembers every now and then, even more so now, in his advancing years.

A stranger gave him water, a stranger and a far better man than he.

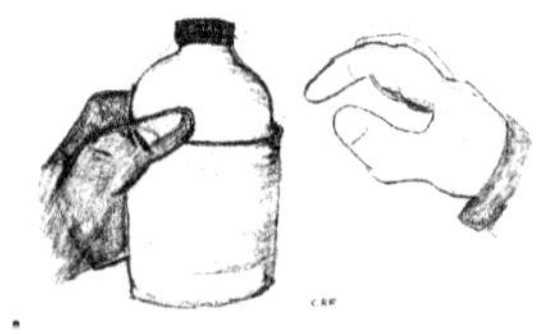

Smiles

There are smiles that make us happy
There are smiles that make us blue

There are smiles that steal away the tear drops
As the sunbeams steal away the dew

There are smiles that have a tender meaning
That the eyes of love alone may see

And the smiles that fill my life with sunshine
Are the smiles that you give to me

By Callahan & Roberts

Good Old *Walter*

Tony knew this guy, Walter, who lived nearby and where Tony kept his automobile in a rent-free garage furnished by an aunt. The garage was not really in Tony's neighborhood, but fairly close; a ten to fifteen minute brisk walk.

Walt and Tony would meet occasionally, and especially when Tony would stop for a cold beer or two on his way home. There was a tap room on the corner of Nichols and Blindana Streets named *The Palm*, owned by a guy named Palmeri, who was seldom, if ever there. There was a neon sign over the entrance that outlined a green swaying palm tree, with the words *THE PALM* painted in black beneath it. It was, Tony supposed, to make prospective customers think of a Hawaiian décor inside the taproom. It was anything but. The owner trusted the operation of the taproom to two spinster sisters, who alternated kitchen and bartending duties six days a week, being closed on Mondays. The sisters lived in a five room flat over the taproom. The Palm was on the end of the street where Walter owned his home, and Tony's garage was roughly in-between both.

Walt was a Polish immigrant, and although he was young when he came to America and did attend school for a very limited time, he never lost his thick Polish accent. But his conversations would often be heavily sprinkled with *dem* and *doze* and *dats* and *des*. If it bothered anyone, neither he nor Tony would care. Why should they? It certainly didn't offend the combination bartender/cook and the regulars. The spinster sisters, however, would not tolerate inappropriate and vulgar language either at the bar or in the taproom. This edict was enforced by the presence of a seventy-five pound German Shepherd named Igor. Igor's sole purpose in life was to protect the two spinster women and maintain peace and serenity in the establishment, and that he did...and did it well. It has been said that a furious bark from this beast would silence even an annoying blaring jukebox.

Late on a Saturday night, or maybe it was early on a Sunday morning, Tony stopped by The Palm for a night cap, and was glad to see Walt at the far end of the bar sitting on his favorite stool. He did not need to see his face to determine if it was Walt, Tony could tell by the span of his back and the thickness of his neck.

With a friendly slap on the shoulder Tony said, "Hey Walt! How are you? Let me buy ya a drink." Walt smiled when he saw Tony, exchange a friendly greeting, and he accepted the offer. Walt had a shot and a beer. Then Tony placed a ten-dollar bill on the bar and told the barmaid, "I'm drinking what Walt is drinking."

When the barmaid finished pouring the drinks, Tony pushed the ten dollar bill toward her and said, "Put one in the barrel for yourself Helen." She nodded her thanks and returned to the cash register to make change. The two men raised their shot glasses, clicked them together, one saying 'nastrawvia', and the other 'saluti', and tipped all of the contents in one quick adroit flicker of the wrist. Then, in the most delicate manner, they picked up their beer glasses and daintily took a half sip. Igor watched from his sentinel post.

The two men then did what all men do at a bar on a Saturday night or early Sunday morning, they talked and resolved all the issues facing mankind. However, in the course of the evening Walt shared a haunting and sobering story that Tony carries to this day. It emphasizes the many stories Tony heard in his childhood from his mother and aunts, his aunts mostly, about *la miseria* in the old country.

It was getting late, and the kitchen had closed a half hour ago. The dining room was empty, the bar was thinning out, and earlier both Tony and Walt had laid another ten dollar bill each, and most of it was now gone. Tony doesn't remember exactly how they got into the topic of immigration and the old country, but he does, and always will, remember the story Walt told, the way he told it, and especially how he looked doing it.

Walt was telling Tony about his life as a very young boy in very rural Poland. He grew up in a two-room cottage. He made certain that you understood it wasn't like the cozy little 'cottages' romanticized by songs and Hollywood. Their cottage had one source of heat for cooking and warmth, and had rationed and limited fuel, straw mattresses, a dirt floor, a door and two windows.

The commune had six cows, and when the evening milking was completed, they were all housed and penned under one roof, abutting Walt's cottage. It was young Walt's chore to get up at sunrise, to go to the pen and deliver the five cows to their owners. The sixth cow belonged to his father, placing Walt's family within one of the six wealthiest in the commune. He and his siblings slept barefooted, and since they shared only two pairs of boots between them, they used them only when there was snow on the ground.

Walt told him that on those cold Polish fall and spring mornings, he would go to the pen and look for the most recent steaming cow's blobbing (stool) and stand in it for a minute to warm his feet. He would then place a rope around the horns of the cow whose owner lived the nearest, and lead the animal to him. He did it in that order (the furthest last and a warm foot bath for each delivery) because he found his feet would be toasty warm by the time he made his last delivery.

At one point in his story, Walt dismounted from his bar stool, and maybe to give a visual demo, showed Tony how hard he would stamp his feet in that cow pen. Igor's ears immediately perked up at the sound of the stamping, and he rose slowly from his resting position and shot a look at Helen the barmaid. Helen was standing by the big black National Cash Register. She half smiled at Igor and quietly re-assured him by saying, "It is all right Igor…it's all right."

Igor slowly drifted back into his prone position as before, but he kept his ears up, as he continued to watch and listen. Tony and Walt both witnessed Igor's action and both smiled. Tony smiled at the dog's action, but when he looked at Walt, he realized big Walt wasn't smiling for the same reason. Walt was absent-mindedly staring at the rows of whiskey bottles on the other side of the bar, all lined up like soldiers at attention, and that far away look in his eyes told you he was really not seeing them.

There are smiles that wipe away the tear drops
Like the sunbeams dry away the dew

Walt is gone now and is mentioned once in a while at The Palm. He was always good for a laugh, and regardless of his size and strength, he didn't have a mean bone in his body. When someone commented on his thick Polish accent, he would admit he was an immigrant but would also remind them he served three and a half years in the United States Navy in the South Pacific on board a destroyer, and his accent wasn't an issue back then.

Tony likes to think, and wants to think, that Walt's *smile* on that night, when he was staring at the whiskey bottles across the bar and not seeing them, wasn't because of Igor's reaction, nor Helen's reassurance to Igor. He was smiling at the memory of how as a little boy he would warm his feet.

Whadda Ya Do With Old Baggage

Tony was just a product of his time and his generation, nothing more, nothing less. Growing up in a brownstone tenement house, with a street full of cousins, aunts and uncles, *commarras* and *koombas*; was a lot different from what was depicted on the silver screen with Mickey Rooney, Judy Garland, and Elizabeth Taylor. Their Hollywood lives were so carefree with short-lived troubles and always happy endings. They all seemed to *live happily ever after,* like fairytales.

When very young it was easy, almost natural, to believe in the Boogie Man who came out only after dark, like Dracula, and the Hook Man who roamed the tunnels beneath Brandegee and Conklin Elementary schools, and bad people who gave you the evil eye…the infamous *Mal-occhi.* There was a whole lot to be frightened of in those days. Good breeding ground for superstitions.

And dreams; those that foretold of terrible disasters (bad ones), or fantastic ones that promised immeasurable wealth and happiness. Tony had an aunt who was senior of all her sisters here in America and who had the God-given talent to interpret dreams and *handle* any mal-occhi situation you encountered. She understood these things… and you loved her, and you believed and trusted her because you knew she loved you back.

In one way or another, you always seem to carry some part of those childhood fantasies and fears well into adulthood—not that you'd believe in all of them—but…it is the baggage you find you can never really abandon.

Shortly after Tony and his family relocated to Pennsylvania, on a quite Saturday morning he and his family where all having breakfast together, when he announced he had a strange (but crystal-clear recollection) dream about a fish. The scales and the quasi-fierce head came to him instantly, but not anything else; like where he was in the dream or what he was doing, an old fashioned mystical mystery, like when he was a kid.

His kids, being young at the time, were wide-eyed and open mouth, as Tony reminded them of their great aunt's supernatural power to interpret dreams and omens and spot envious and jealous people who, while wishing to appear as sincere and complementary to you, were really wishing you ill-fate. Should you ever find yourself in such a situation, you were to put your right hand on your hip…or behind your back (better), straighten and stretch your index and pinky fingers, clamp your thumb firmly over the two other folded fingers in the palm of our hand, and say to yourself, but not aloud…*These horns are for you, you devil. Be gone. Get away from me!!!*

His kids were mesmerized by the story and their great aunt's God given talent, especially the youngest. Tony sat in silence for a minute, bobbed his head a bit, for mystical effect, and then said to the youngest child, "You know what? I am going to call her on the phone right now and find out about this fish!" He left the table and went to the wall-mounted yellow telephone near the stove, with its perpetual entangled, stretched-out, extra-long, coiled telephone cord.

Hello(?)...Hello Zits? (zits was for zia...it was always that way in his family) *Oh sure!!! everybody is good...how 'bout you and Uncle Dan?...Good...good... listen zits I gotta ask you a question...'*

Tony, standing there by the phone and looking at the kids seated round the table, went on to tell her about his dream. You could see he was occasionally interrupted and also sometimes answered in Italian, but soon the conversation was winding down, and Tony was solemn and nodding just a bit. However, just a minute or two before he hung-up, the youngest child saw her father half smile into the mouthpiece of the receiver and just as quickly, returned to the earlier sobering and solemn manner.

He returned to the breakfast table, and by this time even his wife was interested as to what this fish dream meant. And the interrogation began:

What did she say?	*Lots of things*
You know what we mean	*You talking about the fish dream?*
Come on, Dad, quit teasing!	*She had some questions.*
What kind of questions?	*She wanted to know about the fish.*
WHAT? What about the fish?	*She wanted to know if the fish was alive or dead and cooked or raw.*
WHAT? Why did she want to know that?	*I don't know...I guess stuff like that is important to a sorcerer.*

What did you tell her?   *The truth. It was dead and*
raw.

What did she say then? Was it   *Well, she said ...* (He took a
a bad sign? What did she say   sip of coffee at this moment to
help him hide his smile)
'non jew worry..itza not bad!

His wife and sons all laughed at the bizarre logic of the questioning and conclusion, and his daughter (much too young to be cynical) smiled only because she was happy and nothing bad was going to happen.

There are smiles that make you happy

There are several reasons Tony remembers that Saturday morning so long ago, but if he were forced to pick one, it would be the following. You see, he never put too much stock into dream interpretations and meanings, although he certainly knew many people who did, his beloved aunt included. The main reason he remembers is that he knew what the answer would be even before his aunt 'evaluated' the dream. She would never think of hurting him or one of his kids. She just would not.

Something To Be Said

There is something to be said for, and in the defense of, prearranged nuptials. Times and standards and moral acceptance float and swim, soar and fall with the passage of Earth's unending orbits around the Sun. To say, as Charles Dickens once wrote, "It was the best of times and the worst of times..." will continue to echo in the millenniums to come as they were praised or lamented in years past.

In his old age and with his disdain of confrontation, Tony senses a monumental social change usurping current standards and remolding future behavior and norms. He feels he cannot do anything about it now, nor could he do anything in the past. When Tony was in the rat race, he worried about competition and as he was leaving the 'race' the floodgates that held back about fifty percent of the work force (women's movement) was breached.

His main social thought process was to marry (promulgation of the species), be a provider (food and shelter for spouse and children) and run with the competition. He and his wife did the best they could in this environment. We can say 'be careful kids...work hard...do your best' to our kids and grandchildren but not much more. It'll be their generation that has to deal with single parents, gay marriages, test tube babies, genetic adjustments and possibly the end of the institution of marriage as Tony once knew it.

Tony's parents' marriage was sort of prearranged however, both had, as Tony understood it, the right to refuse. The story begins shortly after the end of WW I. His father and three other bachelor friends, all from the same town and all veterans of the Italian Army, came to American by way of Ellis Island. As was customary in those days, bachelors would migrate to a predominately Italian-American neighborhood, would find work and would usually find 'room and board' with an Italian family. During those early years, Tony's father boarded with one of his mother's sisters and brother-in-law who resided on Jay Street, in Utica. By so doing, his father soon met all of his mother's family in America. His father, thoroughly dependable, hard working and well mannered, gained the respect of his landlords and their family. In a five year period he was asked twice to stand as Godfather for their children. The American side of the family knew him as *Koomba* Pete, before it became Uncle Pete.

In 1927, *Koomba* Pete went back to Italy to visit his aging parents and planned to return to America in six months. Tony's mother, then 22 and single, was still in the old country living with her widowed father, her eldest sister and her husband and seven children, in a two room apartment.

Tony's two yenta aunts spoke: *"Koomba Pete when you go back to see your parents, would you do us a great favor and deliver an envelope to our father and sister? It is some money that they can use. We believe it is much better and safer having you deliver it than trust the postal system on either side of the ocean. Our village is only a day and half away from yours, and there is a nearby monastery where you can spend the night.*

"It'll give you an opportunity to meet our family, and especially our youngest sister who is very bright. She can read and write and crochet and she was educated by the nuns. She is in very good health but still un-wed...che peccato...what a sin!"

Tony's father returned to America July 22nd, 1928 with his new wife.

When Tony thinks about his parents' marriage, he does it with mixed emotions. Two needy people, trying to satisfy themselves and not be alone. No walk down a primrose path...no moonlight bay...no shooting stars...just fundamental human needs. If love is wishing more for another human being than wishing for yourself, then it is only time that can prove it to be true .

When Tony's father became seriously ill and required surgery, his operation was scheduled early for 7:30 AM. Tony and his older brother took their father to check in at the hospital the day before, just after they got off work. They tried to make small talk to pass the time, but his father was so tired and ill, he dozed in and out of consciousness. Eventually, he fell into a deep sleep. The brothers made it a point to stop by the night nurse's station to ask if she'd *'keep an eye on Pa'.*

She replied, "I keep an eye on all of them, and I'll make sure he is comfortable for the night."

Early the next morning Tony brought his mother and her favorite niece to the hospital to maintain the vigil. At seven AM, when they were bringing him to the operating room, they passed by the waiting room. Tony heard his mother gasp and sob quietly into her handkerchief, and he saw tears running down her cheeks. He himself turned away and took a deep breath.

"I gotta go to work now, but I'll be back as soon as I can." He paused, and as an after thought asked, "Do you have enough money for lunch and coffee? The lunch room is on the second floor."

"Don't worry about that! We'll be all right," his cousin replied, and Tony went to work.

The operation lasted more than five hours, almost six. Pa was in the recovery room for another three, and he was asleep most of the time. Ma and her niece waited patiently at the bedside, quietly saying the Rosary over and over. Pa opened his eyes, blinked a few times at the electric fixture overhead, turned his head and saw his wife. He smiled at her, and she smiled back.

There are smiles that have a tender meaning
That the eyes of love alone can see

Then Pa told her, 'I have been looking for you.' He reached out his left hand and Ma took it with both of her hands. They held hands, smiling at each other until they took Pa back to the ward. *If love is wishing more for another human being than wishing for yourself, then it is only time that can prove it to be true.*

It was Tony's cousin Donetta, who told him that story. Until the day she died, she could never tell that story without shedding tears.

It Is Those Small Things

Tony's only daughter married and had four children. When the first grandchild was born, it brought Tony great delight and happiness—a euphoria that was only to be multiplied by three and re-lived daily for the remainder of his life.m Grandkids have that sort of effect on their grandparents, sometimes even grumpy old men.

Tony recalls an incident that occurred in his home. His son-in-law and daughter were spending the day and they all were enjoying the first-born who maybe was no more than four or five months old at the time. Tony's sons were also there, and everyone was in the kitchen. The baby was sitting on her grandmother's lap at the table, totally secure, with Grammy's fingers interlaced on the baby's stomach. Grammy made it a point to have the baby's arms free by passing her hands under the baby's arm pits and lacing her fingers as she did, gently pressing the child into her stomach and lap.

The baby was teething, and in spite of that, was in a pleasant mood, graciously accepting all the lavished attention placed upon her. She also made use of the table-top for picking and disregarding various *teething toys* she was gnawing at and occasionally banging on the table to test their durability.

She held court…the baby did…seated on Grammy's lap. To her right sat her mom, and across the table her uncles, all adults were vying for her attention. Her father and grandfather stood directly behind the uncles, both sharing a new and comfortable inner pride. The family had decided, even before her birth, that grandpa was going to be called Pops.

Besieged with various questions and requests, she intermittently chomped on the various teething toys, testing them for soundness on the surface of the kitchen table. Occasionally she would emit *aahs* or singing sounds. A happy scene mostly because the baby was happy.

Say mama...can you say Uncle Pete???...Call Uncle Ray...where are Grammy's pretty flowers??? Do you like the pink ring?? Ugh!!! It is soaking wet with saliva... I'll rinse it...don't throw it on the floor. And then someone asked her...*Where is Pops???*

She was busy banging on the table and watching her handiwork while bringing her left fist to her mouth for a periodic gnawing. When she heard the question, her dark eyes darted quickly to Tony, and their eyes locked onto one another. Tony smiled at her, and she in turn abandoned the urge to chump on her fist, and openly smiled back at Pops.

But the smiles that fill my heart with sunshine
Are the ones that you give to me

All of Tony's grandkids have given him moments like that, and he is eternally grateful to them.

How to Build a Rectory

Way back when Tony was first transferred to Macungie, Pennsylvania, he enrolled his family into St. Joseph the Worker Parish. He could have just as easily enrolled at St. Thomas, both roughly equidistant from his new home. But to him, you see, there was a lot of character that made this small parish so inviting and attractive, especially to his *then* perceived needs. It was a wholesome environment that his family could easily embrace, and even more important that they could quickly be absorbed into and accepted.

And why not? He was first generation American, and his wife second generation American Polish. As he used to enjoy saying, his children were half Italian, half Polish and all American.

The actual church itself was once a one-room country schoolhouse, converted with a proportionally sized added steeple, and located on a road that ran parallel to 'old' Route 22. Today, the new Route 22 merges and divides from a spider web of interstates, searching for Harrisburg and stretching and reaching for far-away Pittsburgh. The first Christmas Tony and his family were members of the parish, they purchased a box of Christmas cards which showed the little chapel-like church brightly lit by flood lights on a wintry evening. To this date, many of the old parishioners can recall the beauty and nostalgia of that simple card. It sort of reminds us, regardless of all those wonderful and inspiring Christmas carols of the season, that there is still a spot, no matter how small, for "Silent Night." Tony loved that Christmas card.

Also back then, there was much, much less traffic, and the rectory was a small framed private residence on a corner lot, facing a quiet street. Its backside was turned against the hustle and bustle of the roaring progress. On the west side of the rectory stood the old former one room school house, now St. Joseph the Worker Church, whitewashed snowy white, with sky blue trim. Continuing west were about ten (Tony couldn't remember exactly) *'boiler plate* or *cookie cutter'* company houses. A shrinking generation will remember the terms 'company house and company store,' especially in Pennsylvania and West Virginia, and recall Ernie Ford's infamous *Sixteen Tons.* At one time those wooden two story double (two family) houses with pitched roofs, were the homes of the families of workers. The fathers and sons toiled at the landlord's cement plant or a quarry, while the apron-clad mothers and daughters maintained the house, and cooked, cleaned and canned. Behind the houses, they kept their little kingdoms of vegetable gardens.

When Tony first laid eyes on those company houses here in Pennsylvania, he recalled an old army buddy from the Bronx. His name was Peter Dolan, and he referred to his neighborhood as Poe Park. We all assumed the name stood for Edgar Allen Poe. He told us there were ten 5-story tenement houses, all in a neat row, on his side of the street. Tony remembered Dolan telling him he had named each for one of the Ten Commandments and he himself lived in the sixth one. As the faiths would have it, the first one to pick-up on the right Commandment was the only Jewish kid in the squad, Donald Ginsberg. *Thou shall not commit adultery.* A snicker and unsavory comments followed, but what would you expect from young boy-soldiers in a barracks atmosphere, with their high testosterone levels?

The St. Joseph community was located in what is still referred to as Pennsylvania Dutch country—Dutchy for short. The old-timers back then had regional colloquialisms such as referring to getting a haircut by saying, "I'm going to get them cut."

Over the years, the community assimilated and diversified, and today may well be considered urban suburbia, as verified by the luxury automobiles in the new church's parking lot. Outside of tap-room humor, you seldom hear that old Dutchy instruction to *throw papa down the stairs his hat*. It was another time sans Audis, Mercedes, and Beamers.

Looking back, Tony now realizes it was really a 'no brainer' opting for St. Joseph the Worker. At the time, he felt he was on his way to the American Dream (or at least how he had visualized it). What the heck, it seemed all his life he was surrounded by men, *the men he knew and loved,* who worked with their hands and worked hard. He was going to work with his head and do better, and he was on his way!

Saint Joe's was a nice place to go, simply because of it's size, its history, the closeness of the parishioners... physically and mentally...the stained glass window— singular—only one...The Good Shepherd with his sheep— not an overwhelmingly large stained glass, maybe even small by most standards...and the statue of St. Joseph the Worker clutching a wood chisel. A good reminder, that is often over looked, Christians follow the teachings of a Jewish carpenter who has become known as the Good Shepherd.

Tony went alone to the old rectory to enroll his family. He does not remember exactly why, but he does remember being alone, and after having been received by the new pastor, he was told he'd have to wait a few minutes. The good *padre* had someone else in his office, and they were almost done. Father Smith was the pastor, tall, lean and ramrod straight, so very much unlike Tony's thick wide frame.

His office was a venture into austerity, an old beat-up desk, a green hooded desk lamp, a couple of four drawer gray filing cabinets, and two cushioned chairs. There was a window with 'old fashion' lace curtains, a picture of the Holy Infant directly behind the desk, and a picture of the Holy Family on the opposite wall from the window.

Tony was relaxed and contented *Yes...three children and my wife...married at St. Anthony's in Utica...the kids were all baptized at St. Thomas in New Hartford...birthdays April 3rd '65, October 7th, '67 and my daughter...October 4th...'71.* Lifting his eyes from the notes he was jotting down, the *padre* said..." *Aah!!! The feast day of St. Francis of Assisi.* "

Tony nodded with enthusiasm...and quickly added..."*and my son, the Feast Day of the Holy Rosary.* "

"I know..." was the *padre*'s reply and they smiled at one another.

Tony thought, "Boy, Ma would really like this priest!!!"…remembering his mother's phenomenal ability to recall and give the history of all the saints Tony ever knew.

And Ma did grow to like this priest…as did Tony himself, his wife and his kids; this tall, ramrod-straight man with a soft voice and a crooked smile. He had the habit of tipping his head to the right and lowering his chin when he laughed or found something amusing. Like the time Tony's very young sons, side by side, brought the gifts to the altar during a mass. Father Joe first accepted the gift of the older boy, turned slightly and handed the gift to an assistant. When he turned back, he discovered that the young brother had started to follow his older brother toward the rear, and HE called them back in *sotto voce*. The brothers obeyed, and the padre took the remaining gift, thanked them and nodded them back to the rear. He had laughed with the crooked little smile and returned to complete the mass.

Eventually, the Parish congregation outgrew the small chapel church, and a new church was designed and erected, and in time, so was a rectory, a parish center, and a school.

Every story has a beginning, middle and an ending. Fast forward through the middle. It is sufficient to say that that young pastor went on to not only complete the building of the new St. Joseph the Worker Parish Church and rectory, but also went on to go on to another community and rebuild still another parish. Tony remained in insurance, and although his insurance career was not meteoric (the Peter Principle just one step ahead of his natural abilities or talents), it placed food on his table and shelter for his family. He is the first to admit that his wife contributed economically, which came shortly after all the children entered school, and it raised their standard of living.

Tony did not lament his mediocre status achievements in his forty years in a business career, but rather found solace in the fact he could always say, *Hey!!! this is still a long way from Catherine Street & that second floor–rear apartment...walk-up cold-water flat...'*

Once, (in that abbreviated *middle portion* of this story) years ago, in the then very new St. Joseph's Church, Tony witnessed what may be considered a small and insignificant gesture. An act...just because of its mere simplicity... made it an act of sincere, unforgettable kindness. Attending Mass one Sunday, and seated off to the far right, Tony calmly and quietly watched the faithful standing in line and then moving forward to receive Holy Communion, cross themselves and then solemnly return to their pews. An old man limped along down the aisle, cane in left hand and further steadying himself with his right on the church pews as he passed, finally arrived at the end of the procession. He looked down to find a solid place to plant his cane and let go of the pew support. He need not have bothered, for it was not necessary. The Pastor had already stepped down from the altar platform, moved to him, stood before him and gave him communion. The Celebrant then returned to the altar platform.

Maybe sharing that scene or retelling it seems trite, but it made a very lasting impression on Tony, because

Tony knew that Jesus would have tried to make it easier for the old timer also. It is something Tony will never forget.

Years and years later, when Tony was in retirement and Monsignor Joe returned to St. Joseph the Worker as a semi–retired pastor, their paths crossed again. Soon, a different and closer relationship of friendship developed. Back when the Monsignor Joe went to Reading, they enjoyed a normal pastor-parishioner relationship. Whether he secretly searched for it or not, Tony had *now* found himself not only a Confessor, but a wise and understanding contemporary.

The church festival is always held in June. On one opening night, the current pastor of St. Joseph was circulating around the various tables situated under a huge rented tent, greeting and chatting with the parishioners and their guests. The pastor, Monsignor Wargo, is a mountain of a man, who pumped iron in his youth, bleeds a greenish-red blood when Notre Dame University loses a game (any game), and grew up in the hills around Williamsport, Pennsylvania with a fistful of brothers. He likes to hunt, too. All this was evident to those he came in contact with and befriended him: He is a soft-spoken man, quick to smile. However, Tony also found and sensed, under that Paul Bunion exterior, a little bit more — maybe like understanding why still water is deeper than running water.

Once while delivering a Sunday homily he mentioned the English author, A. J. Cronin. The name A. J. Cronin sent Tony spinning back into the early fifties, fourth year English Literature, Miss Sue Den fifth period class. And that dreaded oral and written term paper by an author, not picked by you, but assigned by Miss Den. You had to read a minimum of three books by the author, submit a written report on all three and finally give an oral report on your favorite book. If Miss Den suspected you were sandbagging her, the oral report could quickly turn into a Spanish inquisition. There, from the pulpit, almost fifty years later, the good Monsignor mentioned the very book Tony presented his oral report on *The Keys to the Kingdom.*

During Monsignor Wargo's watch at St. Joseph the Worker Parish, the community/campus grew to include a parish center and elementary school and an addition and expansion onto the church itself. The original rectory, built back when Monsignor Joe was the pastor, was built by volunteers. Tony was taken slightly aback when Father Joe told him. A tinge of guilt arose in Tony; he wished he could have been a part of it. But who knows why. Maybe he hadn't even known about it.

Tony expressed his regret for not having participated, and the old monsignor told the old retired insurance man, "Jesus loves us all; He loved Martha as much as he loved Mary." And Tony thought, "Yeah! I gotta remember that."

The Pear Tree

We'll call him Tony, but that is not his real name, and he is a storyteller. Now, well into his seventies and with encouragement from old high schoolmates, Tony has become a storywriter too. He has written a trilogy and refers to it as **_historical fiction_** to enable everyone to become cognizant of literary license, and dabble in prose.

Eugene P. Nassar, Professor of English Emeritus of Utica College, graduated from Keyon College in Ohio, did undergraduate work at Cornell and is a Rhodes Scholar. He is a loyal and proud son of Lebanese immigrants. Tony graduated from high school with him.

The following appeared on one of Tony's book jackets:

Wind of the Land
Eugene P. Nassar
(Mike and Mintaha speaking in their
backyard somewhere in east Utica…circa 1945)

"Ya Mike, our uncle, the pear tree, has
been giving us rich beautiful fruit without a
spot for the thirty-three years we have been married.
And all we do for him is bless him
and fill our bushels. And the plum next to
him is weak and we take the worms from his
roots every year and he does not recover."

"Ya Mintaha, some bear and some do not bear:
some live long and well, and some are
weak and die quick. Nobody knows what
is in the mind of the good God."

<<<.>>>

In one of Tony's bookshelves…about
three or four books in from the left is
Gino's book
…autographed and dated… "in friendship,
Cordially, Gene Nassar …Sept 10, '90"

Once, in conversation with one of his sons, Tony mentioned that old adage…that a painting is worth a thousand words…and the then teenager…simply replied…,"Show me a painting of the Gettysburg Address." Ya, Mike our uncle the pear tree…

Tony's own pear tree reminds him of Gene's parents and their backyard discussion.

The Fig Tree

Along with a very productive pear tree, Tony has (and had) fig trees. Over the past forty years, he has lost, regained and replanted fig trees. The original sapling was given to him by an old Sicilian who migrated to America shortly after WW II.   His name was Don Vincenzo and once you met him, you'd never forget him. Like the Gettysburg Address, if Tony were asked to paint a picture of the *Salt of the Earth,* he'd admit that he could not paint, but would show you a photo of Don Vincenzo and tell you, that he is the *Salt of the Earth* !

Like Eugene Nassar, Robert Cimbalo was also a high school friend of Tony's, and like Nassar taught at Utica College. Bob is an artist. As many of us did after high school, he went into the Army. He served and then attended and graduated from the prestigious Pratt Institute in Brooklyn, studied in Italy and had a studio near the Spanish Steps in Roma.

Bob's artistic contributions to Tony's first two books are much more than outstanding, but what Tony treasures the most is Cimbalo's *Winter Fig Tree.* The following also appeared on one of Tony's book jackets.

Winter Fig Tree
Excerpt from previous correspondence with the artist

I don't think you will mind,
But I visualize your fig-tree painting
Dominating the rear cover of the book jacket.
Interpretation is, I realize, a very personal thing

And to me, what I see…maybe feel would be a better
word…
In this very still, and cold and wintry art piece
Is a combination of a requiem and a promise.

The promise is a reminder of the good things to come…
The hope (*la speranza*) of fruit for your blessed home altar
And a circle of shade from under the relentless scorching
August sun.
Immigrants to severe northern winters know the time has
come to protect life.

November or early December and you find yourself
Trying to tie tight little square knots in pieces of used
clothesline
With fingers numbly cold and achy from the foreign frigid
air
Searching for the necessities of wrapping and stuffing
Dried fallen leaves…some straw…a beat up old carpe…
Maybe even a good size piece of disregarded tar paper
From a nearby construction site. Junk, just junk…
worthless stuff
That promise of food for the table…that promise of shade
from the hot sun…
Those promises seem a long way off, a very long way off
Aah! But what you are really wrapping and stuffing and
binding
Is a dream! that hope, be it little or grand, which in time
Will soon re-appear and in its magnificent way nourish
you.
I love that painting.
It talks to me
And I try real hard to listen

And I try even harder to understand it.

Painting from rear panel of the book jacket for
Wasn't It Only Yesterday (2006).

When telling a story, a storyteller sometimes finds himself painted into the proverbial corner. He doesn't want to leave anyone out, because we are all somebody and God doesn't make junk. We are as much somebody as we are nobody and in this paradoxical mood, Tony penned something like the following in one of his stories.

The Loyal Sons

Enjoying a glass of Chianti and watching the bluish smoke from his Tuscany cigar rise, expand and dissipate, for some unknown reason, (go figure!! how do these thoughts pop up??) he recalled an autograph and written comment in his brother's yearbook. At one time, he considered the quote corny simply because…'you didn't talk like dat' in the neighborhood. 'However, at this time in his life as shadows grow longer, it is different somehow.

He still remembers it:
*'May our friendship be your guiding light through
the dark channels of destiny'*

They were going to take some snap shots and were to meet at Koomba Joe's Restaurant. Joe's Restaurant has become a landmark establishment in Tony's hometown. Two cousins run it, and because they are *farda guingia* (sons of brothers) they were named after their grandfather. You have Big John and Little John. And Big John's father came to America with Tony's father in 1921.

Nick Piperata and his hobby and professional camera…with some arm twisting, he volunteered to take the shots. Tony brought some props. Virtually, at the last minute he realized that one of those wired twisted café chairs which were always part of the restaurant fixtures, should be included. He asked Big John if he could borrow one and John said…"I got one in the back that I can't use anymore because it scratches the new tile. You can have it."

With plastic gliders glued to the bottom of the chair's legs, the chair is now a fixture in Tony's very cluttered *man cave room*. It is only one story amidst thousands that surround him in the room. It is a source of pride for him.

From left to right

Mario G. Fumarola, a storyteller the third son of PietroFumarola fromCisternino,Providence of Bari/Brindisi & Chiara (nee Di Risio) from Vasto, Chieti, Providence of Abruzzi, Italia.

Robert Cimbalo, Illustrator/artist the third child of Santo Cimbalo fromCellara, Providence of Cosenza, Calabria & Rosaria (nee Gigliardi) from Tiriolo, Providence of Calenzano, Italia.

Eugene P. Nassar, Prof. Emeritus of English Literature, Utica College, founder of The Ethnic Heritage Studies Center, the third son of Mikhael Nassar, from Xahle, Lebanon & Mantaha (Minne) (nee Kassouf) from Wadi El Arayesh, Lebanon.

Photo by Nick Piperata

The Glorious Summer and Fall of 1945

The war had officially ended last month in August —- August fifteenth to be exact. Ma let Tony make not only a torch (using his favorite broom stick…sans the straw that once made it a functional broom), she allowed him also to tightly wrap an old beat-up and holey filled towel. Tony and his two cousins, Joey and DB, lit the towel and took turns holding it high. The towel burned completely, and the broom stick was only partially charred on one end. And that was good. Tony still had his favorite toy which in his imagination could be a sword, a rifle, a lance when he was a knight mounted on a charging steed, or could become his trusty rifle with a fixed bayonet.

A month later, in September of that glorious 1945, came the annual Feast Day of Saints Cosmo and Damiano (the weekend closest to the 27th which is the actual feast day). The two Saints are the patron Saints of the village of Alberobello, in the Puglia region of Italy. The village was once in the Province of Bari, but when the Province of Brindisi was added in the mid twenties or thirties, there were changes. Nonetheless, those old timers (a great many of them anyway) from Alberobello that lived in Tony's neighborhood continued to call themselves Barese and to adore, worship, and celebrate their village's patron saints.

The exciting and fun-filled *Festa* weekend would open on Friday night. The streets were closed to vehicular traffic, curbside food stands and game stands immediately appeared on both sides of the street, and on opposite ends of the block two bandstands were raised at least four and a half feet for evening concerts preformed by at least two different marching bands. Electric colored light bulbs… green and white and red and sometimes blue were strung across and over the streets. The lights were attached to long 4 x 4 wooden poles, all painted light blue. When the kids shook the poles near the base, the string of lights would bobble and dance until an adult would intervene. The lights were on from noon to midnight.

The last Mass on Sunday was at noon, a High Mass (with three priests), celebrated on the front steps of St. Anthony of Padua Church. A temporary altar set up at the large double-door entrance was flanked by the statues of the Saints. Draped around their necks, and almost reaching their sandals, was a very long four-inch wide shawl/scarf.
It seemed…like maybe…a half hour or longer… after the outdoor Mass was over, that utter confusion and chaos began to reign. Contingents were scurrying and jousting about…yelling instructions to one another, and no one seemed to be obeying. Somehow or other it began to blossom into a religious procession that would have made a fistful of Roman and Greek gods envious.

Church society's members, women and men, their officers in their Sunday best…had a green, white and red sash draped over their right shoulders. The ends of each sash were pinned together near their left hip. Some of the women wore large picture hats, but the men were hatless. They remained hatless not only because there were priests and nuns in the procession, but because the statues of the two canonized Di Medici brothers followed solemnly behind them —St. Damiano the youngest first and St.

Cosmo, whose statue like face always looked sad to Tony, last.

The pomp and the ceremony seemed to be endorsed by the angels and the saints above; as the sky was ice blue and cloudless. Like a journey of a thousand miles it starts with the first step forward. It started, the church sanctioned society, Saints Cosmo and Damiano de Albrobella stepped out onto St. Anthony Street and headed south toward Bleecker Street. The procession followed a large four by four embroidered drapery cloth of the saints, mounted high on a tall eight-foot shaft, carried by a big, white haired, hatless man who wore harness equipment over his shoulders and at his waist to help support the burden. Two young girls, in their only once worn communion dresses held cords attached to the high-up cross bar of the embroidered tapestry. Behind the slowly swaying tapestry two young teenage girls, with red, white and blue sashes crossing their torsos each carried a large bouquet of red roses. At the end of the procession they would return the roses to the church and place them at the foot of the statues.

Although freshly starched, the white veils the little girls wore would sway gently as the three of them…little girls and the man supporting the tapestry…led the entire entourage into the heart and soul of East Utica.

The first groups immediately behind the society were eight nuns from Our Lady of Mount Carmel Church, only nine blocks away, and the special guest of St. Anthony's Mother Superior, Maria Giuseppi. They were from the same Franciscan order, and their stiff freshly starched bibs and forehead cover contrasted greatly in the bright September sunlight. Tony believes to this day that he has never seen a white as dazzling as those pieces in the habit and shawl of the good Franciscan sisters.

The White Band from Syracuse, a drum and bugle corps, followed. At least one drummer in the three rows of drummers would continue to beat a cadence whenever the procession paused. The Saint Anthony Catholic Youth Organization (CYO) club participated too. Two members carried a six foot horizontal CYO sign. Tall boys in basketball uniforms, and boys in baseball uniforms, as well as girls in cheerleader attire followed behind.

Father Pella from the parish and two other guest priests were directly in front of the tall magnificent statue of Saint Damiano. Three men to every statue would hover around their assigned statue, each with an arm band indicating they were church ushers, and each with a circular Coca Cola or Utica Club tray. The men worked the edge of the procession, accepting money placed in the trays. Should you place a coin or a one dollar bill into the tray you were welcomed to take a small circular lapel pin of Saints Cosmo and Domiano. The pin was smaller around than a fifty cent coin, but bigger than a quarter and some kids had three or four of them pinned onto their shirts.

Occasionally during the procession, someone would tell a tray-carrying usher that he would like to make a contribution of five or more dollars. The procession would stop. The usher would escort the contributor to the front of the statue, the six strong men who were carrying the statue would stop and lower their burden twelve inches so as to enable it to rest upon a sturdy four legged stand. The men would then rub their shoulders and decide if they wished to change sides now or later. A three foot stool would miraculously appear from behind the tapestry that dressed the four legged stand during the procession. The usher would take the bill and pin it onto the sash draped on the statue. Another usher would ignite a cherry bomb firecracker, call for clearance, and drop the firecracker into an empty gallon paint can that had a handle.

The firecracker went off, the boys cheered and laughed, they jolted at the loudness of it and the young girls blinked. Dogs would begin to bark or howl. The paint can and stool went back behind the tapestry stand, the carriers returned to their yoke. On one command, they lifted, and on another command, they started to move forward.

The first half of the procession was mirrored in the second half. (Other church societies and clubs, other church ushers with arm bands and round trays, other firecrackers and statue bearers.)

This was the Saint Cosmo part of the procession.

At the statue's immediate front, was Utica's own marching band...*La Banda Rosso.* When a generous and successful business man contributed twenty dollars or more, it earned not only a firecracker explosion and a short string of lesser size firecrackers, but also a short and rapid rendition of Marcha Reale from the Red Band.

Tony remembered a great deal of events in the summer and fall of 1945, but the most poignant is the memory in which a half dozen or more stout, strong Italian mothers were walking bare footed in the procession. They were carrying their shoes and saying the rosary as the

asphalt road surface disintegrated the bottom of their
stockings, some quietly weeping, and all wearily bobbing
and weaving as they followed the statues of the Saints
Cosmo and Damiano.

Part III

Arts & Leisure

Siena & the Voices of Angels

The Eyes of the Beholder

Almost Poetry

On the Shoulders of Others
Immigration 101
Tony…the Wizard…&…God
Second Floor Rear
White Water Basin

Chiara's Essay

Siena & the Voices of Angels

We will call him Tony, but that is not his name, and he was always a storyteller. Late in life, he evolved into becoming a storywriter. Once he was working on a crossword puzzle and the clue was, *storyteller*, and the four-letter word answer was*: liar.* 'Liar' was verified by the other across and down clues. *Liar* fit neatly like fingers in a glove< but not with Tony.

It fit as things are fit in Hollywood or pseudo-education or politics or mainstream media. The premise is that storytellers are liars. Undaunted Tony forges ahead. It was in Siena, Italy.

Siena

The main square…people…tourist…hucksters…everyone
milling around on
A warm September day… sun in a cloudless sky
Way off on the far side of the square…an audible distinct
sound…a drum?
Yes!!! A single drum beat…a single drum…
cock your head…
listen…
a slow cadence

A distant commotion…over there at two o'clock…a
drumbeat…a slow cadence on
A warm September Sunday…standing in history…in the
past…under a cloudless sky
Now you can see the tips of banners and flags…moving to
the left…and above the multitude
Movement…crowds…you sense people emptying into the
piazza from one of those connecting alleys

The beat of the solitary drum ceases…but
something else…cock your head…strain to listen on
A warm September day under an ice blue cloudless sky
The banners and flags move again… bouncing…floating…
stop…and now they are swaying
Then you hear something…faint and soft at first…the
banners and flags…still slightly swaying
Voices…drifting over the crowd…women's voices…
growing stronger but not losing their sweetness on

A warm September day where…miraculously the sun
wasn't hot
Accapella…the voices fade…applause drifting back…the
banners and flags bounce…and then move on
The drummer again…one beat cadence…you sensed…you
knew something special was coming

Anticipation…they are coming…plant yourself here…
needn't move…the parade will pass here on
A warm September day under pale ice blue sky and a
festivity enjoyed by all
We position ourselves…They are coming…they'll pass
right here in front of us…the drum beat nears
The banners and the flags are being carried by…the
drummer comes into view…renaissance costume

The drummer stops…the procession fans out…men dressed
in costume…like masterpiece painting on
A warm September day under blue skies and over cobble
stones that St. Catherine tread upon…
Male voices…loud and deep…their chins up…bellowing to
the sky…accapella too…you can see in their
Faces…with their bodily gestures…they loved it…and they
sang more for themselves as for the mob

On queue…the renaissance men stopped…turned 180
degrees…and melted into the admiring crowd on
A warm September day under icy blue skies and upon
blessed cobble stones that saints walked upon…
As the men were absorbed by the multitude…the mob
surrendered a group of renaissance women…
Fluttering initially…forming a semi-circle…inter-locking
their fingers beneath their breast…they sang

And were joined by children in costume…who held each
other's hand…for safety, confidence
and love
On a warm September day…the sunlight…like the breath
of God…equally
Warming the cheeks of the cherubs, and the grapes ripening
in the mountain vineyards of Tuscany
Drawing the sweetness of the angelic voices and the sugar
to the grape
Then there was applause…fluttering of renaissance
costumes…flags and banners raised slightly on
A warm September day in Siena…on a beautiful September
day
The drummer struck the tight skin of his drum…He stepped
off…the flags and banners swayed and followed
The renaissance attired troupe stepped off smiling and
nodding to the clicking cameras of the multitude

By hand, head and arm gestures…children were corralled
into walking in front of the women on
A warm September day that must be like what Heaven is
like…
The children moved…talking, giggling, occasionally
skipping…the little girls still holding hands

Tony and his brother exchanged the usual… *"How about that!!!"* and *"Whadda show!!!"* Both were equally impressed. Still, within the sound of the distant drummer, Tony's wife came to him and asked for the camera. She informed us that they (she and our sister-in-law) were going to follow the procession. She told Tony why.

Hasty plans were made… "Why don't you and your brother go to that café over there and have an espresso or something…we'll be right back!!!"

"It is all right with me…We'll find an outside table…and will be waiting for you two to come back."

"Good…we should be back in a half hour or so." And off they went.

Tony and his brother found a table after about a ten-minute wait, sat down and ordered: two espressos, and two grappas. Then they settled in to do some serious people-watching. At one point in this leisure and comfortable pastime, Tony's brother asked where they were going. He had not heard what Tony's wife told him a few minutes ago.

Tony likes his espresso with a sliver of lemon peel to rub the lip of the demitasse cup and swig of grappa, and before he answered his brother, he sipped the espresso, swallowed, took a sip of grappa and let it stay under his tongue for a minute. His brother was watching him, not sure if he had heard the question.

Tony warned his brother not to laugh…and told him because….they may sing again…

And for some unknown reason he now wishes he had gone with them. How many stories can a storyteller absorb in an afternoon, under a cloudless September sky?

The Eyes of the Beholder

Tony will try to thank the many people who have always helped and encouraged him in his old-age adventure into storytelling. But first, however, he'd like to share a historical comparison and then a very ironic coincidence that occurred just as he completed the final draft of *The Last of the First.*

The ironic coincidence regards a book published in 1943, and the historical comparison involves two renowned French artists in 1869.

History tells us on the banks of the Seine in the summer of 1869, two young French impressionists…Monet and Renoir "…both set up their easels every day"*… maybe sometimes side by side, and applied their craft. There by the river water, and upon canvas, with their brushes and oils and their sense of color and feel for light, these masters painted the same scene. The pieces exist today and are **both** titled *La Grenouillere.*

Over many years there have been times when Tony would be in a light mood, would say something like… *Yeah!!! I got something or other **just** like that…but **different!*** The oxymoron might create smirks in adults.

Monet

Renoir

<u>BUT,</u>

that is exactly the way Tony felt after he had already completed telling his story of the *Last of the First* and then reading William Saroyan's, *The Human Comedy*. Tony the storyteller and author William Saroyan have their own *La Grenouillere*. Tony does not wish to provoke the ghost of the son of an Armenian immigrant who wrote a great masterpiece in 1943, but wants to re-assure him this story is as Tony saw it and believed in it.

Because Saroyan's work came to him after he had completed his own story telling, Tony feels he cannot 'acknowledge' it, Instead, he wishes to point out the coincidences.

Tony acknowledges his family (*la famiglia*) and Gino and Roberto and Anita and the many friends (*li amici...e anche...li amici di amici*) and thousands of characters he has come to know and then love or hate and respect and, most of all, learn from over the many years of reading.

MONET: His Life and Complete Works by Sophie Monneret Longmeadow Press 1985

Almost Poetry

On the Shoulders of Others

We all stand on the
Shoulders of others…
Those who came before us…
We must stand erect and strong
…not only for ourselves…
…not only for those who support us…
…but…
For those who are yet to come

Immigration 101

The immigrants soon learned that
The streets were not paved with gold…

They…and their children…did learn
That if pride was a venial sin

Then shame must be a mortal sin
Because shame destroys the spirit

Tony…the Wizard…and God
(SENZA MUSICA)

A crowd…a huge noisy crowd
had gathered in front of the Wizard's drawn curtains…
"Silence!!!" he roared…
and then again… *"Silence…!!!"*
The crowd became silent.

"Who speaks for this wretched mass of humanity?"

"I do" someone answered

"What is your name???"

"Tony…my name is Tony…"

"Who are you???"

"Nobody…I am nobody…"

"Who are those people behind you???"

There's Paulie…and Donetta
There is Fridone and Finnocchi
My mother and my father,
My brothers, my two sons
My wife and my daughter
My aunts and my uncles
My cousins from Catherine Street
The folks from Koomba Joe's Restaurant
The eight people from the Feast…
The Jimmy Western bean picking gang

My first grade class…
Miss Bailey's fifth grade class…
The coffee drinkers from Carmen Caruso Café
& the Florentine Pasticceria…
The shoeless women who follow the statues of the Saints
saying their Rosaries…

The old lady with the push-cart…
La Banda Rosa…Patsy the chicken man…
The workers from the textile mills
with lint in their hair

"Enough!!! Enough!!! What do they want???"

"Nothing!!! niente!!! They want nothing.
I just want God to bless them."

"All of them? The good, the bad, the ugly???"

"All of them! The long, the short and the tall."

"There is a lotta junk in there!!!"

"There is NO junk in there!!!"

*"Whadda ya talking about Tony? I see lots of junk in
there!"*

Tony… "There is NO JUNK in there!"

"You are wrong, Tony. And I won't bless them!"

"I don't want **you** to bless them Wizard!   I want **God** to
bless them.
YOU…Wizard…are just like me!
A fictional character…just paper & ink.
But not these guys behind me. **They are real!"**

They laughed…they cried…they sang…they loved…
dreamed & wished…
And they are not junk…I am asking God to bless them
all!!!
The good…the bad…& the ugly
The long…the short…& the tall!!!

ALL OF THEM!!!   *TUTTI!!! TUTTI!!!*

*Tony believes that the two hundred and ninety one words of
the Gettysburg Address are one of the most moving
selection of words in the English language. He has heard it
delivered with and without musical accompaniment. The
impact of the meaning and the actual message of the words
remain unchanged to him.*

TONY...THE WIZARD...&...GOD
(CON la MUSICA)

A crowd...a huge noisy crowd
had gathered in front of the Wizard's drawn curtains...
"Silence!!!" he roared...
and then again... *"Silence...!!!"*
The crowd became silent.

(Hush little baby ...don't you cry)

"Who speaks for this wretched mass of humanity???"
"I do.." someone answered
"What is your name???"
"Tony...my name is Tony..."
"Who are you???"
"Nobody...I am nobody..."

(I got plenty of nuttin)

"Who are those people behind you???"

There's Paulie...and Donetta
There is Fridone and Finnocchi
My mother and my father,
My brothers, my two sons
My wife and my daughter
My aunts and my uncles
My cousins from Catherine Street
The folks from Koomba Joe's Restaurant

The eight people from the Feast…
The Jimmy Western bean picking gang…

My first grade class…
Miss Bailey's fifth grade class…
The coffee drinkers from Carmen Caruso Café &
Florentine Pasticerria
The old lady with the push cart…
La Banda Rosa…Patsy the chicken man…
The workers from the textile mills
…with lint in their hair

(Hail…Hail…the gangs all here!!!)

"Enough!!!   Enough!!!   What do they want???"

"Nothing!!! niente!!! They want nothing.
I just want God to bless them all."

"There is a lotta junk in there!!!"

"There is NO junk in there!!!"

*(Said the shepherd boy to the mighty king
…Do you know what I know???)*

*"Whadda ya talking about Tony? I see lots of junk in
there!"*

Tony… 'There is NO JUNK in there!"

"You are wrong, Tony. And I won't bless them!"

(Everyone is beautiful...in their own way)

"I don't want **you** to bless them Wizard!   I want **God** to bless them.
YOU... Wizard...are just like me!
A fictional character...just paper & ink.
But not these guys behind me. **They are real!**"

(No man is an island...Entire of itself...)

They laughed...they cried...they sang...they loved...
dreamed & wished...
And they are not junk...I am asking God to bless them all!!!
The good...the bad... & the ugly
The long...the short...& the tall!!!

ALL OF THEM!!!   TUTTI!!! TUTTI!!!

Hush little baby...I got plenty of nuttin' from Porgy & Bess
by George Gershwin
Hail!!! Hail!!! The gang's all here!!! Beer Barrel Polka
by Jaromir Vejvoda
Said the shephard boy to the mighty king...
by Gloria Shayne and Noel Regney
Everyone is beautiful in their own way... by Ray Stevens
No man is an island...entire in itself essay
by John Donne (1573-1631)

Second Floor Rear

Sixteen steps…a spindle railing…the third spindle
From the bottom
missing…since God knows when…
it was always
kind of dark at the bottom step…
the double- hung window at the top of the landing
provided light.
On a sunny day you had
to squint when you looked up
…and you climb the sixteen steps…
Sixteen steps up and out of the darkness.

Reproduced through courtesy of
Robert Cimbalo

A Note from the Storyteller:

Catalonia is a green, somewhat leafy vegetation with a tubular stalk and leaves that resemble dandelion leaves in looks and in taste. The catalonias have this name because the region of Catalonia is known for what is sometimes called "asparagus chicory." It is sold in bundles which resemble how asparagus is sold. Although the catalonia bundles may often resemble asparagus, they do not taste like that vegetable. Catalonia was a commonly used table vegetable in southern Italy, and it naturally found its way to the immigrant's table.

They were often tossed in salads (with vinegar) or boiled/fried with olive oil and garlic. Should you have seen catalonia growing in a field, in all probability you would disregard it and consider it only a pesky weed.

As children, sometimes we would strip the outer leaves, snip the crown, and use the stem as a straw. It seemed to enhance the ice cold glasses of Seven-Up we had at Sunday dinners and even more so, if Pa changed the color of it with a splash of his wine.

White Water Basin

She would place the fresh cut catalonia into an oval two-
gallon, painted white porcelain water basin.

The bundles of catalonia were tied in tight little circles.
They stood on end like soldiers at attention.

She would find a place for the basin somewhere on her
two-wheeled push cart.

Maybe between the cucumbers and tomatoes.

She then poured about three inches of water
into the basin.

If you were to ask her why, she'd reply
"To keep them alive."

And the kids all believed her…

Even though they knew the stems were cut
from their
roots.

Chiara's Essay

We will call him Tony, but that is not his real name, it just helps Tony to relate. He is an old man now. He is also yet in another *stage* of life:

There have been numerous stages over the many years. Even in his retirement, Tony went through stages... escapes to Florida to avoid the snow...depending more on 'volunteer' help in planting garlic and winterizing the fig trees...much of his outdoor activities shrinking...quietly slipping into indoor activities...computer...cooking...his little work bench in the basement... and sometimes even television.

When in the safe, warm, comfortable confines of his kitchen...where everything has a place or should...where it is either just right or just about right...and your senses filled...hearing the sizzle ...smelling the freshness...seeing the juices...touching/feeling the texture of food and materials...sensing the heat...the kitchen table... EVERYTHING...is a manifestation of family and food to him.

To a first generation child who was too young to remember with clarity of the thirties and the depression... but heard so many stories of the hardships from loved ones, he came to believe and accept as gospel...the kitchen table was holy...like a church altar.

No one argued at the table, the conversation was civil, friendly, educational, and informative or there was none.

Tony was in this fuzzy-warm mood one afternoon when his wife told him his daughter had called and told her one of the kids had written an essay. It seems the school was commemorating National Grandparents' Day and the class project was to write an essay about their grandparents. His daughter had asked if Tony would like to read it. She had made a copy for him, and he could pick it up whenever he wanted to (like Tony needed an excuse to go and see the grandkids!).

Grammy & Pops
By Chiara Huber
Christmas Tradition

My grandfather always says the two most important things in life are family and food. Both of these key pieces of Italian lifestyle come together on Christmas Eve at my grandparents' house. When we arrive at Grammy and Pop's house on Christmas Eve, one of the first things we do is go into the basement with Pops to get measured. There's a wine rack in the basement that has all our heights measured on it since age three.

Our Christmas Eve dinner comes from an old Italian tradition, The Feast of the Seven Fishes, which originated in South Italy and was upheld by the Roman Catholics. So, every year we have seafood for dinner on Christmas Eve. When everyone is finished eating, we are finally allowed to open our presents.

Grammy gets everyone seven or eight presents each year, one of which is guaranteed to be pajamas. For as long as I can remember, Grammy has given each of us a new pair of pajamas for Christmas. Once all the presents are opened, the kids (my sisters, brother, and I) change into our new pj's for the annual photo. This photo (taken by my dad) goes into a photo album kept by my grandfather. These annual Christmas photos go way back to when my mother was a teenager.

These simple but fun Fumarola traditions fill our Christmas Eve, a highly anticipated night filled with family and food.

Tony can remember other Christmas Eves, and smiled to himself, feeling satisfied with life.

He remembers his father's big strong hands and thick wrists, and how he would open the clams and then place them on a tray. He remembers Pa cutting little x's or crosses in the *castange* (chestnuts) and placing them into the oven to roast. Tony's eldest son has hands like that!

Tony remembers his mother…with her small delicate hands …patiently and efficiently stuffing the *calamari* (squid) tubes, then placing them into the sauce to be cooked and later to be served over linguini.

Tony considered himself fortunate because his other son took more than a passing interest in the preparation of stuffed *calamari*. He literally learned how at his grandmother's knee. She was a small woman from Abruzzi on the Adriatic Sea. Old man Tony believes his mother and father are and will be at his table every Christmas Eve in spirit.

Tony's greatest source of joy is his grandchildren, and his favorite holiday is *la Vigilia* (Christmas Eve).

He recalls Chiara, the eldest, with her big, beautiful dark eyes flashing and laughing at life as **she** sees it, and at other times sad and pensive. But always...always...intelligent, conveying "Yes, I understand."

Little Mia (not so little any more)...with a smile that seems to tug just a bit on the right side of her mouth and then bursts into a full fledged thing of beauty like a rose. It seems it is always Mia who seeks him out, comes to him, kisses him...saying a simple...*Hi Ya Pops*...& then they hug.

Then there is Anna. Even at a very young age she showed signs of being the most family-oriented. But it was she... little baby Anna...who convinced Tony that the saying *nothing is beautiful at birth*...was not always the truth.

John is Tony's only grandson. John's father is a hard-working professional. Tony is quick to tell anyone that they don't come any better than his son-in-law. The grandkids adore him, and each vies for his undivided attention. That is a lot of completion for a young boy, and when his dad is working, John's home environment is dominated by the other gender. There…at Pop's house…he can find BB guns, fishing poles, big uncles and firecrackers, all of which are a great thing for a ten year old boy.

A recent incident reinforces this observation. From an assortment of scraps on his workbench and a recyclable 7.5 ounce sardine can, Tony fashioned and made a toy German Tiger tank. Young John helped by painting the tank gun-metal gray and the finished product looked as good as a Hollywood prop.

One Sunday afternoon, grandfather and grandson decided to test it; six shots from the Red Ryder BB gun (3 each) moved it only a smidgen. They carefully planted and lit three firecrackers beneath the tank…but, other than the flash and noise—no damage. They then decided to place a firecracker *inside* the turret and under the hatch door to see what would happen.

Then the strangest thing happened! The entire turret—the 88 millimeter gun, the hatch cover, the antenna—blew straight up into the air…two feet…and crashed into pieces. Then two kids…one not yet ten…the other not yet 78… vowed to start a new tradition, only this one for future New Year's Eves.

It is love of family and food that always returns.

Tony's mother's name was Chiara.

Part IV

Puzzles & Comics

***Reader's Digest* Rejects 3 for a $1.00**

The Factory Workers

Go Figure!!!

A Better World & Your Contribution

And Now?

Two Thoughts

Reader's Digest Rejects
Three for $1.00

Reader's Digest #1

Sudoku and Arms/Finger Dexterity

This was another candidate piece that Tony considered sending to *Reader's Digest.* But he never did. He has since re-read it and thinks that maybe he should reconsider.

Our newspaper has now included the Sudoku puzzle. The first day they ran it, they stated an editor completed the first puzzle in 19 minutes. The day after, the paper reported the feed-back regarding better times than the editor. The best time was under 4 minutes!

The newspaper has a 6 column format, and the Sudoku puzzle is placed directly on the center crease.

The next morning, I told my wife, it took me that long to re-crease the paper to work the puzzle….but…I'm getting better…I can now refold the comic strip in less than 2 minutes!

Reader's Digest #2

Tony thought it was a good story. He got a lotta laughs with it at parties…and bartenders always liked it. So he decided to send it into *Reader's Digest* as a "**Life in These United States**" item.

Tony diligently worked on the text (*RD* has a word limit on such submissions), massaged the words, fixed the punctuation and finally submitted it electronically.

…and like the man who got onto the Boston Subway
system who never returned…
it was lost in the galaxy
of cyber
space………………

Airport Security

With the normal pre-flight jitters and anxieties I arrived at JFK ready to fly to Sicily. Immediate concerns: check-in the luggage, then security, with maybe a pit stop in between.

Two of three done, onward to security.

The line moved slowly, until, "Next!"

I placed my carry-on onto the belt, emptied my
pockets into a container, and waited.

The attendant caught my eye, with a slight
   downward bob of his head and said (*sotto
   voce*), "Your zipper."

Whoa!!! "Whadd'ya want my zipper for??"

He explained, "I don't **_want_** your damn zipper.
   Your fly is open!"

Reader's Digest #3

Years ago, when poor Tony had to go for a colonoscopy, he was abruptly made aware of how norms have changed, especially in communications. The fading Victorian Era manners and decorum (which was his moral compass in dealing with the world around him) had been washed away by time and by the streamlining of daily norms.

But on with the story.

After obediently following the doctor's written instructions and consuming an ocean of a not-too-savory liquid the day before, Tony found himself sitting on a gurney on the fifth floor of a hospital prep room. He pondered if anyone…any one at all…ever felt comfortable in those chin-to-knees-tie-in-the-back-pajamas they give you prior to surgery.

Soon two nurses (one young, the other not too much older) appeared, had him lie on his back, jockeyed the gurney round and pushed him through the door. Off they went rolling to the antiseptic prep room. In the corridor one of the nurses asked if Tony had any questions.

With a tinge of embarrassment, and in spite of the foul tasting liquids consumed earlier and the effect it had on his digestive track, Tony expressed concern that maybe his lower track was not totally vacated The senior nurse replied, "Don't worry it'll be fine…and they have a vacuum right there if needed."

He looked at the lighting fixtures as they flew by overhead; as he wished 'this' would all be over and done with. Soon enough, he found himself waking up in the same recovery/prep room and staring at permanent lighting fixtures: it was over, thank God.

The escorting nurses reappeared and inquired how he was feeling. He was asked to stand to prove his stability and balance, which Tony dutifully did. However when he swung his legs over the edge of the gurney, his body passed gas. He felt terribly embarrassed since it happened in the presences of two young women, and he quickly attempted to apologize.

The older of the two young nurses replied with a smile, "No need to apologize, it is music to our ears." As the two were leaving, the younger nurse drew the curtain around the gurney and said, "You can get dressed now."

While dressing, Tony thought just how 'old fashion' he was; but, on the other hand, if 'that' was music, he was glad to be tone deaf.

The Factory Workers

The Onieta Knitting Mills were all on Broad Street, as were the Mohawk (Utica Sheets) Knitting Mills, the Skenandoa Cotton Company and the Foster Brothers Mattress Factory and several other industrial structures. The mills were all multi-story masonry (brownstone) and although not abutting one another, if you stood on Broad Street and looked directly east or west, the factories and mills gave the appearance of a long high protective wall. A single railroad track siding ran parallel to the mills like a castle moat. The automobile parking lots for each building were smaller than those you now see for bank branches or drugstore chains; they were much more than adequate to accommodate the very few automobile parking spaces needed in those days.

The vast majority of the working forces for all these establishments walked to work. There were bus stops —an east-west line—two blocks up on Bleecker Street…but the direction, and sometimes the cost…at times made the ride impractical.

The textile mills and factories developed and coordinated an audio system of gathering their flocks. It was in twilight days of coal-fired steam engines that drove power staffs and leather belts and heated water and nagged workers with the shrill call of the factory whistles. The whistle routine may have varied with many mills, but nonetheless, it was the Oneita Knitting Mill routine that Tony became mostly familiar with.

The first screeching alarm from the Onieta was 5:55 AM. The first shift had five minutes to get to work. The next time the whistle screeched was 6 AM, and your time card now had only three minutes of grace. After 6:03 there would be deductions.

Again, at 6:45 AM the whistle spewed a white puffing compress cloud out of a tiny orifice to alert the 7 AM shift. It was a reminder it was a work day. *Are you awake yet?* Then at 6:50 it loudly and forcibly asks you again.

Another blast at 6:55, to tell women and men …but mostly women …*you gotta hurry up ...you gotta leave your home...you gotta go to work*!!! Because he lived only two and a half blocks away, Tony's father would leave on the fifty-five whistle. In the alley way he would balance his lunch pail under his arm and he would light up his Lucky Strike cigarette.

By the time he got to the factory gates, he would drop the cigarette, step on it and enter the factory door directly under the NO SMOKING sign. There remained but one more whistle blast.

Some, but certainly not all of the workers, liked to be early; some would arrive early enough to have to wait to punch in — the sign on the wall by the punch clock ordered: *do not punch in till after 6:45.* The activity…the queue at the time clock in the AM was like a twinkle…a forest rill in the late fall…no longer fed by the melting snow of last winter…that may carry a fallen leaf … slowly…from here to there.

There were whistles at high noon every workday, in all probability for lunch.

The last whistle from the textile mills was at 3:30 PM. Then like hemorrhaging the blood of the mills and factories, workers gushed out onto the streets. A stream… thick and controlled…would scurry out of the exit doors of the mills.

All seemed to move quickly…like they had places to go…or were needed elsewhere. The further they got from the exit portals, the thinner the stream became. Due south on Kossuth Avenue the stream of workers would flow, clusters would turn right or left on Catherine Street, others at Jay Street and right or left onto Bleecker Street (a few stopped to wait for the buses at the bus stop).

The thinning would eventually lose amperage, and the eager step-falls would slacken a smidgen. They were getting closer to home, and suddenly their bodies reminded them, that they were weary from work. They only had so many more hours before the screeching steam whistles would call them again.

As a boy, young Tony would sit on the wooden stoop of the house where the Scatina family lived. The first floor was retail/commercial, a social club and a small banquet room in the rear. The second floor had two apartments, one of which the Scatina's occupied. Tony would quietly watch the crowd flow by, always looking toward the mill to catch sight of his father. Once he found him, he locked his focus on him until he crossed the street.

Tony would then jump off of the stoop and run to meet him. He liked to hold his hand and walk home with him.

Go Figure!!!

The trilogy was completed. It pleased Tony to think that he could do it. At the same time, it forced him to realize just how much help and support he needed. He had always suspected he might be one of the worst spellers to ever graduate from Brandegee Elementary school. His grammar and diction were not that far behind, maybe even sometimes overwhelming.

The final book in the trilogy was *Last of the First*. It still totally boggles his mind as to how the faiths destined this E-mail to come into his computer. What are the odds? What are the chances? Go figure!

E-mail from Geraldine

We will call him Tony, but that is not his real name, and there is no reason for calling him Tony other than he is much more comfortable telling his story in the third person. 'It' being a true story.

Tony has written a trilogy about growing up in east Utica and growing old far away from the old neighborhood. With some 'enlightenment' from an old Army buddy, he now describes the trilogy as *historical fiction*. But is it?

Tony's old neighborhood was anchored in the east by St. Anthony of Padua Church and in the west, by Our Lady of Mt. Carmel. Roughly, the two churches were ten blocks apart (east/west) and both were off of Catherine Street. Kossuth Avenue (north/south) was the dividing line for the churches' parishioners and Brandegee Elementary School was near Kossuth.

Just before Thanksgiving 2012, Tony received an e-mail from an Amazon customer regarding a mix-up in a postal mailing address. Geraldine, the sender, explained she wanted a copy of *Wasn't It Only Yesterday* sent to her elderly aunt who still resides in Utica. Geraldine, who now lives in North Carolina, explained she thought her aunt would be thrilled to read it because she once not only lived on Catherine Street, she even lived in the Melchiorre House. The Melchiorre House, a gray, twelve family, three story frame structure, was adjacent to Brandegee School.

The Melchiore House!!!

Tony could not believe his eyes, but there it was on the computer screen: *'She lived in the The Melchiorre House on Catherine St. during the time period of your book.'*

The Melchiorre House!!!...The Melchiorre House... of all places!!!

What a shock. Tony absent mindedly waved his opened left hand...palm up...then suddenly stopped and stared at it.

And there!!! the thumb...St. Anthony of Padua
    Church
And there!!! his little finger...Our Lady of Mt.
    Carmel Church
And there!!! his trigger finger ...the brownstone
    tenement house he grew up in
And there!!! ...the longest finger...Kossuth Avenue
    and Brandegee School
And there!!! ...the wedding ring finger...the 12
    family frame Melchiorre tenement house
And there!!! ...in his wrinkled...once callused...
    now soft palm... his neighborhood
And there!!!...he is reminded of the altar boys'
    response, when at the beginning of Mass
    the priest would say,*"I go to the Altar of*
    God."

And there!!! in the innocence of days long gone …
the altar boys would respond
*Ad deum qui laetificat juventutem meam….To God
the joy of my youth.*

The Melchoirre house was painted a sober gray, and in Tony's mind, it was always sort of melancholy and sad, like the month of November. November starts with All Saints Day, and then All Souls Day, and then Armistice Day, and it can be cold and the sky can look like the color dirty gray-black lead. The days get noticeably shorter and there is that crisp heavy scent of snow that Tony imagined he could really smell.

November, when Ma and Pa would fret and worry how they were going to pay for the blue anthracite coal needed for the forthcoming frigid cold. They were not alone in this apprehension. Their thoughts and the thoughts of all the neighborhood parents always crept back to those dark, dusty coal bins in the basements of the tenements and how much coal was contained therein.

November reminded them that the number of nice warm sun-shiny days would be shrinking and erased in the months to come. There is Thanksgiving, the third Thursday. "We have a lot to be thankful for, and we have a ton of coal in the dusty bin in the cellar."

The last book in Tony's trilogy talks about the Melchiorre house and about two War Department telegrams delivered there. *'Last of the First'* page sixteen:

If The Melchiorre house was a 'she' and if she could claim all the families…the men who worked digging for road crews or working in a steaming dye room, who left early and came home late and hungry; their women raising children saving a penny here and a penny there, sewing torn overalls and mending socks, and happy because this was so much better than the misery in the old country; their noisy little kids, the older kids who spoke prefect Italian to their parents and also perfect English on the street and started to learn about sex, the life and hustle that lived and died within her bowels and her soul—then She, The Melchiorre house would tell you she sent thirteen of her boys to far-away lands to defend democracy.

She sent thirteen of her beautiful flowers and the joy of her youth to defend her, and others, because "my country 'tis of thee."

When Tony was researching the various families, he found that one family had three sons and three daughters. All three sons went off to WWII: a paratrooper in the Philippines, a GI at Bastogne, and a Marine on an island in the Pacific. All three received Purple Hearts, one posthumously. Telegram one.

Ironically, (if that is the correct word) within less than a decade, there was another flower lost, this one in Korea: Cpl. Joseph D. Melchiorre. They called Joe 'Firpo', and he went to high school with Tony's older brother and they went to the senior ball with their girl friends…Dorie & Babe. —- Joey died in North Korea, by the Yalu River. He was a POW, and he died of malnutrition. Telegram two.

Telegram one: LOTF (*Last of the First)* page 51…
"A Melancholy Refrain"*)*

They say that *la signora* Parteleo was never ever
really the same after that fateful May afternoon. Her
youngest son, with his flashing jet black eyes and his curly
hair and his happy disposition…his quick…friendly and
sometimes teasing smile…was dead. He had died on a
piece of land in the middle of the ocean far, far away called
Okinawa.

Telegram two: LOTF page 157…Circa 1950-51…
Korea…Joey's death

And once again his eyelids lifted…revealing a
dying fire, and his thoughts were of Dorie and the
Miraculous Medal she had sent him for his birthday…

That fire now was just a bed of embers. His head
was resting on his shoulder near the top of his forearm,
and for no reason whatsoever he tried to cross himself
with his free hand. *In the name of the Father, and of
the Son, and of the Holy*…his eyelids darkened his
vision, but this time he knew they would not be lifted
again…not in this world anyway.

November is a melancholy month. It conveys a sort
of separation. The Church wants you to remember the
dearly departed souls of the dead, and to pray to all the
saints in heaven and to also remember that the Advent
Season is upon us, and the joy of Christmas is near. The
Government has decreed that the third Thursday is

commemorated as a day of Thanksgiving. The Government also sanctions and endorses parades and flag waving for veterans. Tony looked at his left hand again and saw the separation.

The Melchiorre House has long been razed, but the churches are still there, offering daily Masses to the faithful. Tony's old three story brownstone is still there, and Kossuth Ave still divides the parishioners (but Brandegee School is now Brandegee Apartments). Tony sips his wine and half smirks, thinking that a finger has been amputated, but it was there at one time and it was part of a living neighborhood.

Still brooding, Tony asked himself, *In another ten–twenty years who is going to know about The Melchiorre House and the old neighborhood?* He drained his wine glass and suddenly smiled very broadly. *YES!! YES!!! Some will know.*

He reached over and picked up a printed copy of the e-mail he had received in late November 2012, and he continued to keep smiling and felt better.

You see, this Geraldine also lived in The Melchiorre House. You see, it was one of Geraldine's grandmothers' sons who never returned from...*a piece of land in the middle of an ocean far, far away called Okinawa.*

You see, it was Geraldine's mother that named her daughter after her brother Jerry, who died on...*a piece of land in the middle of an ocean far, far away called Okinawa.*

A Better World and Your Contribution

Tony has met with moderate success as a storyteller-storywriter. The reason he prefers storywriter to author is that he believes the word 'author' is rooted in the word 'authority'. He knows, he is not an authority on anything whatsoever! Further, the expression *moderate success* is akin to the word average; which is the best of the worse and the worse of the best.

So, wrapped in this blanket of insecurity and indecision, he forges ahead onto a plateau that he cannot rise above nor go below. He is cognizant of his numerous short comings but still believes and wants to say, *"I have fought the good fight"...Timothy 4:7*. He will neither apologize nor insist. He will attempt only to be an honest witness and observer of recollections. Tony is a product of his time and the clock started on a sunny warm Thursday in March 1935.

He has been told it was a beautiful spring day and that on that day half the neighborhood was out sweeping and cleaning their front stoops on his beloved Catherine Street.

Excerpt from Tony's speakers notebook

(Intro for male and female readings for *Immigrants All!!!*)

Immigrants All!!!

We all know April Showers bring May flowers…
And the Mayflower brought…pilgrims
Times change with or without immigrants and pilgrims

When I was in the first and second grade, we were taught to
write only with a pencil…
Upon entering the third grade we started to write with pen
and ink
In the upper right corner of the desktop was a small circular
hole that contained an ink well
Left handed kids had to reach over to dip their pens
Or… had to learn to write right handed

My left handed granddaughter goes to junior high school
today
WITHOUT
a pen
a pencil
a book or paper.
She goes to school with a computer.

Mind you now!!! These changes occurred in *my lifetime!!!*
What changes are coming in our grandchildren's lifetime?
Everything changes and nothing changes.
Immigrants will always still want things to be better for
themselves
and
certainly better for their children.

Tony wanted to remind his audience he was and
remains, only a product of *his time*. The listener and the

reader are also only products of their time: All of us know time ends and starts on the other side of eternity.

Even living and being and witnessing...*his own time*..., he remains totally in awe and overwhelmed by this electronic age...its speed...its volume...its accuracy. The last time he was home...Utica...he stopped for a red light on Genesee Street, and from his vantage point he could see the Utica Public Library, a structure that always impressed him. Although time has left some aging signs, it still remains a solid, complete building containing with all knowledge learned over the years by great minds. It was the factual counterpart of a Roman Catholic which housed spiritual understanding and mysteries.

The library, wide and squat, shows six large arched windows on the first level, a grand double door entrance flanked by two ionic Greek columns a flight of concrete steps, a circular drive, and remnants of a cast iron fence with cement posts closer to the street. There are six windows immediately above the large arched first floor windows, which allow more light into the structure. They are rectangular, smaller than those below it, and are not arched on top.

In those hallowed walls, Tony always believed, was all of human and not necessarily spiritual, knowledge. Today...all that...can be carried in your pocket in the form of an iPad or something comparable.

The street light then changed to green, and Tony moved on.

And Now?

Truth be known, a while ago Tony commandeered his youngest son's bedroom and proceeded to convert it into his *man cave*. It was ideal; a large rectangular horizontal double 36" by 72" window which opened to the south. Should he have been just a smidgen of artistically inclined, his retirement life could have been painting masterpieces with oils and pastels. The lighting was perfect.

There was however, still another prominent feature — a cork bulletin board. It ran the entire length of the wall, corner to corner, eighteen inches down from the ceiling and four feet up from the floor. Back in pre-historic times when Tony's son occupied the room and way before the bunk he had at Camp Lejeune, the boy had tacked up some items such as

a world map up in the corner,
a newspaper photo of the Blues Brothers
(Dan Akroid and John Belushi)
a pompous photo torn out of a book showing
Benito Mussolini in an orator posture,
a photo of his Pop Warner football team,
a couple of personal photos taken when he stood
for and as a young godfather
to a baby cousin, three times removed.

It is a memory bank he seldom visits. Aah, but Tony …Tony cannot say the same thing. He literally lives in the cluttered 'cave,' and has covered the cork board with his documentation of history.

In the upper left hand corner of the bulletin board, the world map is now almost entirely covered, buried under clippings and photographs. The corner is dominated by three different 8 ½ by 11 inch pictures. They are tacked on, almost forming a sort of triangle with the apex being a young woman depicted in the final stage of launching a javelin at some sort of track and field event. It was one of the very first board attachments Tony made.

Somewhat below and to left of the javelin thrower is a computer-generated black and white photograph of Tony's parents. It is one of Tony's favorite pictures of them.

His father shows a gentlemen's crop of graying hair. He is in a suit, with tie and monographed handkerchief neatly tucked. He looks straight into the camera's lens and does not smile.

His mother does not yet show gray hair. Her hair is combed straight back and worn in a tight bun, not seen in the photo. She is smaller than her husband and wears a dress Tony still remembers seeing in one of the two small closets they had in their flat on Catherine Street.

Neither one is smiling or frowning: both look back at you contented, both neither wanting nor asking you anything whatsoever. That photo (circa 1948), as evidenced by its placement on the cork board, has been there quite some time. It covers a portion of the right leg of the javelin thrower, from the knee down.

The third 8 1/2 x11 was taken from the back cover of a hospital/medical magazine and is promoting physical fitness. It depicts a young…strong…determined…woman who is running. Her long stride almost makes her muscular legs appear to be parallel to the ground. Her black spandex running trunks, snug on the thighs and hips, end at the knee, revealing a bare solid calf. She wears no socks, as if emphasizing her toughness and determination. She has on a sleeveless wine colored tank top shirt, revealing the healthy flawless skin and muscle tone of her shoulders, neck, and arms. At the end of each arm, her very tight fists pump her forward, the left totally bent ready to move rearward, the partially open right elbow starting its swing forward. She has her hair in a pony tail and does not appear to be sweating. But what mesmerizes Tony about the picture, is the hostile, determined and demanding look on the young girl's face. That photo too, covers a little bit of the javelin thrower's picture, her left leg from the knee down.

In a short span of twelve to fourteen years, Tony's little corner collage of womanhood expanded and went from then what was considered by him as a spoof…or a humorous challenge of male masculinity of a girl heaving a javelin to the sanctity of motherhood to…move over…you are in my way!

He is glad to be out of the perceived race. He is comfortable in his domicile surroundings, with his wine and a good Tuscany cigar. Competition is no longer a factor in the equation (his equation). His race…to whatever people race to…is over.

Tony hopes that when he was a participant, the pounding of his running feet loosened and dissipated hatred and fear of anti-Semitism and racism. He feels, "We are only slightly different and certainly not enough to make us hate or fear. It is so much easier to try to understand and respect others' point of view with the dignity you want them to show you."

We…human species…are supposedly 'pack' animals, similar to a family of a wolf pack, a pride of lions, a community of primates. Trust and security overshadow and nudge at competition and egotism, out of its realm. As humans we are further endowed, through thousands and thousands of years of evolution, with a special gift of being able to touch each finger with our thumb.

This physical ability probably enabled mankind to come down from the trees, and to bravely bring fire into our caves and eventually, maybe even help plant seeds.
Tony half hopes that in the run, his pounding feet did not loosen nor dissipate the dust of loyalty and the enduring sense of family and food.

Some things take time…lots of time.

Two Thoughts

Two thoughts gleaned from the same proverb, and a Jewish proverb at that! The first and the third books of Tony's trilogy have very similar openings and somewhat different closing thoughts. They are printed on the book jacket's rear flap of *Wasn't It Only Yesterday* and *Last Of The First*.

The first thought is that he (Tony) tries to tell the reader about how *it used to be,* fearing that the forthcoming generation will forget, or worse, not even know. The second thought is about your *state of mind*: and how you coped while living your own life. It's not necessarily what you think you want that'll make you content, but what you do with what you have.

Wasn't It Only Yesterday (book jacket)

I've advised that a picture of me and a little blurb as to why I wrote this would be in order, and may (some say) be interesting and helpful to the reader.

This brings to mind a Jewish proverb that goes something like: "With a full purse, you are wise, and you are handsome and you sing well, too!"

A full purse, of course, translates into "rich", and rich is relevant. There is Bill Gates and there is a man trying to raise his family, living in one of the shacks that ring Mexico City. To the former, I must be miles below the poverty line; to the latter, I may be the owner of Fort Knox.

To share still another thought on relativity, the size and weight of my overweight aging body is somewhere in between the size and weight of the nucleus of an atom and the size and weight of the Milky Way galaxy.

Who am I to write something? (*Smart kids write books! You ain't smart!*) An admonishment echoes far back in my brain, "Who died and left you boss?" The reply is always the same, "Nobody!", or in a more rebellious mood, "Who sez I can't? I wanna give it a shot."

To me I am a rich man who has a purse, thinks he can be wise, believes he is handsome and sings almost as good as Sinatra. Maybe I can document the way I saw things and leave it for my grandkids to think about…

How are they going to know about brownstones, metal lunch pails, the various uses of a clothes line, or winterizing a fig tree, and all the other good stuff?

How dey gunna know?
Whooze gunna tell'em?

Last Of The First (book jacket).

Thinking again of my favorite Jewish proverb *With a full purse, you are wise and you are handsome, and you sing well too!*

I am as rich as I need to be, and sometimes I think I might be a little wise, and sometimes I think I might be a little handsome, and sometimes I think I can sing as good as Sinatra. It is a state of mind.

Of late…my thoughts have been those of any old man…content in his retirement and in awe of the present and bewildered by what the future holds for the kids.

There is however, something deep inside me that wants to tell the 'kids' about the old days. It is possible that maybe not their generation, but certainly those that follow, who won't know what a brownstone is or what a cold water flat is or what a twelve family tenement house is, and what it was like to live, and love and die in that environment. The old neighborhood was anchored on the east and on the west by two Catholic churches and had a public elementary school (Brandegee) in the center.

Looking back, the separation of 'religion and state' was civic, physical and physiological. I think a lot of us grew up believing and trusting in both science and medicine, but until they could answer all the questions we knew there was something on the east and west sides of our little world.

Part v

Epilogue

Requiem of a Storyteller

Epilogue

Requiem of a Storyteller

When I was a child I spoke as a child...
1 Corinthians 13:11

(Racial & Feminist observations)

Recess time was over. The bell rang. The kids re-entered the school by age groups and gender; first, second and third grades. The outside proctors of the recess session would line up the students accordingly, trying unsuccessfully to quiet the cackling and giggling girls and at the same time round up the older boys who would still be running around the school yard. Eventually, the children would enter the school through the designated doors, the girls the 'Girls' entrance, and the boys via the 'Boys' entrance.

The teachers would meet their respective classes and march them downstairs to the restrooms: boys on the left, girls on the right. Other than the gym teacher, industrial arts teacher and the principal, the other teachers were female; it was the WWII war years.

The female teacher would accompany the girls into the restroom. The boys were met by the school janitor, Mr. Lux, standing with crossed arms and as big as a mountain by the boys' restroom. He was rumored to always be carrying a foot-long rubber hose (a rumor he and others never really denied).

The boys quietly marched single file to the huge upright urinals to relieve themselves or not. Nevertheless, all were required to wash their hands afterward.

Tony and his two new friends, Joey Dellasandro and Jimmy Moore, shared the spigot and a block of rough 'brown soap' at a deep mop sink to wash their hands. They then took one paper towel apiece (…watch out for Mr. Lux's "You're not to take more than one…") and worked at drying their wet hands.

Jimmy Moore, who was black and had recently moved to Utica from Georgia, lived on Jay Street, two blocks from Joey. Tony noticed the palms of Jimmy's hands and they were as 'white' as his…just the palms and the 'face' of his fingers. He asked Jimmy to show Joey…and he…like Tony…marveled at the white palms. Because Tony thought their recent hand washing made Jimmy's palms white, he asked Jimmy, 'Why don't you wash the rest of 'ya self with dat soap? Don't ya wanna be white???"

Jimmy paused and then answered, "I don't know." After all these years, Tony still wonders what question he was answering.

There was a time, back in the old days, when on Saturday afternoons kids could see a double-feature movie …and more…at the neighborhood theater, (the *Family* on Bleecker Street and the *Rialto* on Nichols Street). They would include at least two cartoons, *Movietone News of the Week*, and a serial/chapter (*Flash Gordon, Captain Midnight, the Green Hornet*, and so on).

On occasion, the movies would also have a sing-along feature. It seems strange to Tony today that he and the other kids considered those sing along songs comparable to golden oldies of this generation. Truth be known, some of Tony's generation consider them to now be classics. The 'sing along' film reel would run the lyrics across the bottom of the screen with a bouncing ball to synchronize the lyrics with the music and the chorus.

"Let Me Call You Sweetheart"…
"On Moonlight Bay…"
"I Want a Girl Just Like the Girl **…"**

By today's music standards, there is not just a mere generation gap between the two…no…there is a generation schism…a deep abyss.

But that's all right…it was a different time. A girl friend was a sweetheart…your imagination created Moonlight Bay in your seven or eight year old memory bank…and you really could almost hear banjo's strumming. Tony's favorite remains "I Want a Girl…."

Strong ethnic Mediterranean family culture revered motherhood, and songs like that only tended to reinforce the devotion to *la famiglia.* It was a truism to Tony and his contemporaries. If marriage was in our future it had to be: to a good old fashion girl, with eyes of blue…and the only girl that daddy ever had, (when and if challenged, the eyes of blue were optional).

The kids sang it with gusto and believed in every word…it was honest and as true as the Gospel.

I understood as a child, I thought as a child

"Did ja see dat African Tarzan picture-show where those big tall natives …in da jungles… where dey were dancing around dat big BIG kettle with a fire under it???"

"Did 'ja see how long dare spears were??? Dey were dancing around like crazy in the middle of the night getting ready to throw dat guy into the kettle and cook him and eat him ???"

"Dey was cannon balls and they used to eat people!!!"

"Dey wasn't cannon balls…dey was called cannibals…but ya know too…dat not only dem seven foot people live in Africa, but dem little pygmies do too!!!"

"Your buddy Jimmy is a negro ain't he?"

"Yeah so what??? He ain't like them…he don't come from Africa. He came from Georgia with his mudder and fadder to pick beans and now dey live here. Jimmy lives on Jay Street by the public bathhouse near Mount Carmel Church."

Tired-looking people, mostly women with lint in their hair, seemed to gush out of the textile mills when the three thirty steam-whistle screeched and gave permission. They all hurried to the sanctuary of their homes. Tony remembers one in particular that sadden him. She had a club foot and appeared to have to struggle just to keep up. She was a short woman and was Polish. He knew she was Polish by her fair color and that she turned left onto Catherine Street and walked toward St. Stan Polish National Church on Nichols Street.

His peers also noticed her, and on one occasion a hypothetical catastrophe was discussed and someone asked the question "What would you do???"

"What if the mill started to burn and she couldn't get out???"

"I'd go home and get a blanket soak it and put it over my head and go in and get her out!!! Like that cowboy did in the movie when the barn was burning."

"Whadda ya do if dare was a flood on Broad Street…a hundred feet deep…and nobody learned you how to swim yet…what would you do???"

"I'd run home and cut all da clothes lines from da back windows…knot dem tighter than anything to make da rope a mile long and I would throw one end of it across

Broad Street to her, and she could hold onto the rope and I would pull her across da water. Dats what I would do!"

But, when I became a man, I put away the things of a child

A life time later, on or about the time of Tony's fiftieth high school class reunion, Tony renewed a friendship with a classmate from a different neighborhood. His name is Don, and he is a lifelong friend of Eugene Nassar, and like Gene, he, too, is Lebanese-American. Don reminds Tony of his older brother; a sober, intelligent, no-nonsense guy that looks you straight in the eye. You could say he was almost the opposite of Tony, with Tony's sometimes flippant ways and moods. Nonetheless, Tony got to like him (maybe it should be re-like him) and made him his Utica emissary.

Since the class reunion, Tony has come to learn a great deal more about his hometown ambassador. For instance, he spoke only Arabic before he was enrolled in kindergarten class, and he had one older sister. He did well in school. He worked part-time for Coca Cola, and after graduation he went full time. Don lost his father when he was seven, and his mother was only thirty five years old when widowed.

Our high school guidance counselor was a soft-spoken gentleman named John Moses. He was Lebanese-American, born in Utica. He attended Utica Free Academy where he graduated Valedictorian. Later, he attended Hamilton College and graduated Valedictorian there also.

It was Mr. Moses's experienced keen eye that recognized Don's academic potential, and he campaigned diligently. Finally, both mother and counselor convinced Don to go to college. Don graduated from Rensselaer Polytechic Institute near Albany with a metallurgist degree, and later obtained a Masters in Mathematics.

But this is not about Don; no, it is about his widowed mother who worked for forty four years at the Oneita Knitting Mills. Unbeknownst to either, she too (like the many others… with lint in her hair) marched quick-time past Tony as he was sitting on Scatina's stoop.

And if he could, Tony would have thrown a wet blanket over his head and run into the burning mill to save Don's mother and the little old lady with the club foot.

And if he could, Tony would have run home and cut all those clothes lines and made a rope a mile long and thrown an end over the 100 foot deep flood to save Don's mother…and…the little old lady with the club foot.

Tony would if he could but he cannot. He does, however, often say a Hail Mary for the eternal repose of their immortal souls and hopes that they now rest in peace. When he thinks of them the words serenity, dignity and quiet respect, embraces a much more profound meaning.

Tony and Charlie, an old army buddy, often reminisce electronically about past Army experiences, one of which was a dreaded detail while stationed in Germany. First and foremost, of which, was the infamous Ash & Trash. It was the most cursed and humiliating detail ever concocted by the 8th Division Headquarters. The blood of all the enlisted men of 12th Infantry Regiment, turns cold and soon becomes iced.

At Monday morning formation, each company, including Regimental HQ, sent two squads minus squad leaders and cadre, to center 'Quad'. There they were met by cadre from division HQ motor pool and five duce and a half trucks with drivers. The men were assigned to their trucks and warned that not only the driver…but all of them were responsible for returning the vehicles clean and washed.

Then the five trucks left the Quad area, and like dung beetles rumbled off into all the various regimental areas…to fill and empty its bowels several times. It started at 0800 hours and the details rarely returned by 1800 hours. Their company mess halls always left two cooks and the entire KP detached on duty to feed them dinner.

The company billets (old German barracks) were still heated by fossil fuel. In the winter months this 'ash' factor was the biggest negative. Tony still remembers how, after lifting and shaking an ash receptacle free of its' packed contents, the whitish-gray dust would envelop the entire bed of the truck.

It wasn't too much better in the summer, when you faced and endured the heat and the stench of rotting garbage. All the enlisted men had at least two sets (or more) of fatigues (uniforms) as to enable them to have clean attire for the rest of the week.

Martin Luther King was assassinated in Memphis. He was in Memphis to support the garbage collectors union. The union members were striking for a pay increase. If memory serves Tony correctly, the daily wage was one dollar. A grievous injustice and unfair salary for what was asked of the workers. It was a humiliating insult to the dignity of any man.

Tony remembers his first grade friend Jimmy Moore. He remembers Jimmy's reply to his question: "Don't you wanna be white?" Tony also remembers Pvt. Stanky, a black kid from Alabama, who willing and unselfishly shared his canteen and nodded his approval when Tony silently requested another swig.

There, deep down in his memory bank, Tony can still see their eyes and sense their demeanor. It leaves him with the image of his parents' photograph in his office. Serenity, dignity and quiet respect that make you embrace the meaning of the words more profoundly.

I have fought a good fight. I have finished the race.
I have kept the faith
2 Timothy 4:7-8

It is quiet now. His mind is no longer darting… jumping… from here to there. If there is more to say it'll be short or an idea on a wadded piece of paper at the bottom of the editor's wastebasket.

I have fought a good fight.

Nonetheless, Tony's eyes keep returning to the three photos on the left side of his wall-to-wall cork bulletin board. The two athletic young women—one heaving a javelin, the other running in full stride, with a determined look and ready to take out any two hundred and seventy pound linebacker that gets in her way. Go, Girl…show me how strong you are and show me how far you can throw a javelin…if you want.

I have finished the race.

The other photo is of his parents, taken more than sixty years ago, neither smiling nor frowning, both serene and content…asking for nothing…wanting less. They, like us, did not know the wonders the future holds and like us…

…have kept the faith.

Tony knows he is not superior to any man, regardless of race or religion and tried to live within the boundaries of social and religious teachings. Tony also learned that there was…and probably still is…a generation of women, who endured more than he could ever handle. They…those of yesterday, _women with lint in their hair,_ and their counterparts of today, are no way lesser human beings than he. No, Tony has come to accept them a notch above equal.

CPSIA information can be obtained at www.ICGtesting.com
Printed in the USA
BVOW06s0629170716

455836BV00002B/3/P